The Fire and the Rose Are One

By the same author

The Crucified Jesus is No Stranger
God is a New Language
The Dreamer Not the Dream (with Kevin Maguire)

The Fire and the Rose Are One

SEBASTIAN MOORE

THE SEABURY PRESS • NEW YORK

1980
The Seabury Press
815 Second Avenue
New York, N.Y. 10017

Printed in the United States of America

Library of Congress Cataloging in Publication Data

Moore, Sebastian, 1917–
The fire and the rose are one.

1. Jesus Christ—Crucifixion.   2. Christian life
—Catholic authors.   I. Title.
BT450.M59   232   80-17730
ISBN 0-8164-0468-2

Grateful acknowledgment is made to Harcourt Brace Jovanovich,
Inc. for permission to reprint excerpts from "The Dry Salvages" and
"Little Gidding" in *Four Quarters* by T. S. Eliot, copyright 1971 by
Esme Valerie Eliot; and from "The Hollow Men" in *Collected Poems
1909–1962* by T. S. Eliot.

For
Illtyd Trethowan

With the drawing of this Love and the voice of this Calling

We shall not cease from exploration
And the end of all our exploring
Will be to arrive where we started
And know the place for the first time.
Through the unknown, remembered gate
When the last of earth left to discover
Is that which was the beginning;
At the source of the longest river
The voice of the hidden waterfall
And the children in the apple-tree
Not known, because not looked for
But heard, half-heard, in the stillness
Between two waves of the sea.
Quick now, here, now, always—
A condition of complete simplicity
(Costing not less than everything)
And all shall be well and
All manner of thing shall be well
When the tongues of flame are in-folded
Into the crowned knot of fire
And the fire and the rose are one.

T. S. Eliot
"Little Gidding"

CONTENTS

ix

Introduction

This book represents a new stage in an inquiry, pursued for at least twenty years and now second nature, into the meaning of the crucifixion of Jesus.

Two controlling questions disengage themselves. First, how is Jesus in his climactic moment *recognized* by us? This breeds a nest of questions: What are the elements in our experience that we must single out so that we may recognize them, and thus ourselves, in the drama of Jesus? These elements are obviously our salient features, but what shows them to be this? Is it our own introspection, or the story of Jesus, or both in an interaction to which an implicit faith holds the key? The second controlling question is: Where should the interaction between the story itself and reflectively understood human experience be studied? Should I consider what goes on when I, or any other Christian and especially perhaps a very much developed one like Teresa of Avila, contemplate Jesus on his cross? Or should I conjecture what went on when the different political-interest groups of Jesus' day confronted his challenge? Or should I seek to identify with the experience of Jesus' followers, ask what went on in them? The place of interaction to be preferred, the person or group to be imaginally privileged, will be the one in which the event elicits the deepest and most enduring things in our nature. Only thus can the event be made much more recognizable by us.

These are the two questions: What do we look for in ourselves by which to recognize Jesus, and where do we look for it in the story past or present? These two questions have been working on me, for most of the long period of search, in a very confused way. Neither question was adequately formulated, nor was the distinction between them adequately observed. God knows how they ever got themselves together, met and finally worked together. It seems that not only does the heart have its reasons which reason does not know, but even the mind has its obscure thrust towards order that is the last thing the mind will be able to point to, to name and to control. Very slowly the two questions came out of their manipulative hiding place, became distinguished and were addressed with some order.

The answer to the first question was: Work and work, and go on working, till you have identified and named one universal human desire without some satisfaction of which our life would be unendurable, and total satisfaction of which would be perfect bliss. Work till you have identified and named one universal trait that is the counterpull to this desire.

My strongest formative influence here was Ernest Becker (*The Denial of Death*),[1] who points to the obvious as only genius can. He made me conscious of the passionate sense of self-worth which characterizes human existence everywhere. 'We are hopelessly absorbed with ourselves.' The positive element I was looking for had to be this sense of self-worth in its fully articulated form, which is the desire 'to be myself for another'. I reached the slogan: 'That we all desire to be desired by one we desire is the one uncontested human proposition.'

The negative would be the direct opposite of this thrust towards a generous selfhood. Quite independently of this line of thought, I had been fascinated for a long time with the idea of guilt as an ultimate forlornness, isolation, withdrawnness. Then it clicked. This sense of forlornness, so deeply ingrained in everyone, *was* the sense of not being for the other, of failing the other: was, in other words, the 'opposite', the anti-eros movement, for which I was looking. To recognize ourselves in the Jesus story would be to see at work, in some ultimate confrontation, our radical desire and its canker, our radical guilt. The story would be the story of the liberation of the desire from its crippling and inwoven companion.

Then came what was perhaps the crucial discovery. Why do we want to recognize ourselves in Jesus? Is not this the last word in narcissism? To answer this question, we have to probe more deeply into that fascination with ourselves which creates our desire 'to be myself for another'. If we look at this fascination not, as Becker was

---

[1] *The Denial of Death* (New York: Free Press, 1973 and Collier-Macmillan).

constrained to do, within the limits of the Enlightenment and its prescribed agnosticism, but in a more whole and simple way, a question can spring up. If I am intrigued and excited by my being, to such an extent that I recognize in this passion something that is in all people everywhere and in every time, what must my real feeling be towards one who knows and wills that by which I can only be intrigued and excited? For this feeling, 'dependence' is a churlish and colourless word.

This feeling, could I but be in touch with it, hungers to hear, from that 'one', that I am precious in his eyes, just as we experience in our relationships the supremely human 'desire to be desired by one we desire'. We desire that 'one' with all the passion of our existence. This desire seeks consummation in the Yes of the Beloved. It is guilt, our deep sense of isolation and forlornness, which dulls this desire, instilling doubt and hopelessness of ever knowing that we are, in our ultimate cosmic reality, loved.

There, born fully grown like Minerva, was my Christology. Jesus, our existence without guilt, is able to hear unimpeded the voice of the Beloved: You are my beloved in whom I am well pleased. With this secret, which shapes his whole way of being in the world, Jesus lifts people up to hear in their hearts, in their fellowship and in the whole world of nature the Yes of the Beloved. With the failure of his mission, and in its bitter conclusion on a cross, he plunges them from this height into the original emptiness, the death of God. Coming to them again, *then,* in that awful gap in time, he is God, he is life, he is the unlocking of the Spirit, he is that Yes of the Beloved over which death, the great human pretext of guilt, has no more power.

Lifts whom, plunges whom, comes to whom? This is our second question. There is only one possible answer, for there is only one group who had all three experiences, of lyric, desolation and eternal life: the followers of Jesus.

The stage was set for a full psychological appropriation of the story of Jesus. The outcome has been so amazing that I felt compelled to choose the rather presumptuous title this book bears. The results are the opposite of reductionist, whatever the word for that would be: above all the recovery of the belief in the divinity of Jesus *as* the Holy Spirit's principal therapy of our spirit. As a Catholic I have always held this belief, but theologically it existed for me in that peculiar osmosis with its early conciliar formulations which is one of theology's worst contemporary ills, its symptoms apparent alike in the conservative and in the progressive.

The effect of liberating my belief in the divinity of Jesus from its virtually exclusive dependence for meaning on the Nicene formula was that I appreciated the formula for the first time, both as to its limits and as to its necessity for faith. There is nothing paradoxical here. Limited to the intellectual sphere, this huge truth about Jesus chafes, becomes sore and is consequently avoided. Both the truth and its intellectual ('Hellenistic') habitat come to constitute a single unpromising area. But with this truth rediscovered as the truth that frees the heart for God, the conciliar formulation becomes the appropriate witness of the intellect to this liberation of the heart. Moreover, with the heart at peace with God's truth one becomes more intelligent. A sort of reverent myopia clears up. One sees that he who was experienced as doing for us what only God could do must *be* God.

This mutual invigoration of speculative intelligence and the heart is fundamental to the Catholic theological tradition. Would that we could recover it! We do work that way. The way from the resurrection encounters to Nicea is the good way. If we have built for centuries on the denial of that weddedness of mind and heart, what is there to do but in some way to begin again? It would take the most exquisite engineering skill to add a storey to the leaning tower of Pisa, but what's the point? We seek a new modernity, a flowering of ancient wisdom that would sharpen our awareness of ourselves in the world we now inhabit. This is the place for me to acknowledge Bernard Lonergan as the master in whose school I have known something of this priceless awareness, as undeniable by him who has it as is the enjoyment of Mozart. We should surely expect that the transformation of the person in Christ would show up in the intellect as well as in the heart, and especially in the intellect's enlarged capacity to name what is in the heart.

Another effect of beginning to recognize and to appropriate the experience out of which the New Testament was created has been a renewed sense of the vital role of the Holy Spirit, at least to the extent of sensing the vertiginous imbalance consequent upon the comparative neglect of the Holy Spirit in theology. I hope this book represents a plateau, not just a foothold; and that it may prove spacious enough to accommodate a few readers.

Finally, I have many friends to thank, both in the Marquette community and outside it, for their continual support in my somewhat eccentric labours. They have given me a love for the U.S.A. which I cannot put into words. I owe a debt of special gratitude to an English friend, Peter Harvey, of the Queen's College, Birmingham, who read my manuscript several times and found many places where the presentation or the logic was weak. He thus saved this book from being needlessly opaque. I am privileged to have such a sympathetic censor. It is like having a weak left lobe reinforced.

PART I—EROS

1. A Theological-Temporal Map

Theology is the sustained attempt to understand religious experience. Literally, talking (Greek *logos,* the word) about experiencing
God (*Theos*). Similarly, biology is the sustained attempt to understand (*logos,* to get a good *logos* about) life (Greek, *bios*). We can
trace this venture through four phases.

1. Patristic. Fathers of the Church. First eight or so centuries.
Telling the story of human salvation, using all the art of the story-
teller, imagination, myth. St Augustine's massive *City of God* tries to
interpret human history in the light of the story of salvation. Imag-
inative, poetic, mythic material found in the old Greco-Roman
culture was used to exemplify the story. That world had myths. A
myth is something basic in human experience in story form. The
perpetual experience of death and new life finds expression in the
myth of the dying and rising vegetation god, Tamuz, Adonis. The
desire to enhance both the world of the living and the world of the
dead was expressed in the myth of Orpheus journeying through
the underworld. So Christ was presented as the true Adonis, the
true Orpheus. This phase might be called a Christian baptism of
ancient pagan myth. This period saw the formation of the main liturgical texts. Telling the story in all sorts of ways.

2. Scholastic. A new need creates a big shift, the need to question, to reason. Telling the story is followed by asking questions.
What do we mean by the words 'God', 'sin', 'salvation', 'grace',? At
this time (twelfth to thirteenth centuries) the texts of Aristotle became available to the west, through the Arabs. The brilliant Greek
attempt to construct a rational universe (fourth to third centuries
B.C.) is now carried out in the context of the Christian story of salvation. 'The medieval synthesis.' Aquinas. Making distinctions, as
reason loves to do, e.g., between the knowledge of God we can have
by thinking about the world and the knowledge we get from revelation. Or between what we can do to be good by our own powers

and that for which we need the grace of God. All catechisms are profoundly influenced by this phase.

3. A huge new question. No longer 'What is the story?', no longer 'What does the story mean in terms of the rational mind?', but 'What does the story mean in terms of human self-awareness? What's it *like* to be "lost", to be "saved"?' The coming of the self. Luther. Beginning of the modern world.

This third phase becomes very complicated, for human self-awareness is inexhaustible. Eventually we are no longer content with a stereotype Christian self, a Christian Everyman. There are different experiences of being human: the black experience, the feminine experience, the experience of oppressed people, and others. Hence different theologies: liberation theology (third world), political theology (our world), women's theology.

This bringing to awareness of more and more groups reaches a saturation point. Consciousness, trying to take in the different issues of oppression and justice, becomes overloaded. Too much is claiming our attention. The whole movement of human liberation has to explode into a new unity at a deeper level. Thus we are beginning to find the next phrase.

4. A new phase trying to be born, based on the search for a deeper unity in all human experience. Is there some state of being which everybody wants? Becker belongs to this phase of our culture. Note that theology moves along with the movement of culture; the theologian is a person of his or her time and place.

I am trying to create theology in this fourth phase. I am trying to tell the original story no longer in terms of myths, no longer in terms of its rational implications, no longer in terms of different human experiences, but as the story of the real self in all people. Therefore I shall interpret the experience of the followers of Jesus as the story of the real self in its three stages: of awakening to the wonder of God (the Galilean Springtime), of the death of God (crucifixion), of rebirth (resurrection).

It needs to be added that this theological-temporal map is simplified to an extent which might understandably irritate the professional historian. It is no more than an attempt to pick out, albeit impressionistically, certain dominant characteristics of each major phase of the history of Christian thought, in order to gain some idea of where we are.

4

2. The Search for the One Thing Needed

The first distinction we have to establish is that between sensation and feeling. Sensation is a response to an external stimulus. Feeling is self-awareness. The most effective way to point to this sharp contrast is to give a list of sensations and a list of feelings which a class of fifty people produced in five minutes' recall. That virtually all the states classed as feeling-states clearly belong to a category distinct from the comparable list of sensation-states indicates that the distinction is readily available to introspection. We know, quite clearly, these two distinct worlds in our experience. Here are the lists:

Sensations
burn itch scrape hungry hot cold wet dirty pain tired stuffed cramp tingle sweaty warm drunk exhausted high sick nauseous thirsty burned-out hung-over numb smothered cramped weak full sore crippled sticky energetic injured muggy strong sleepy envy stinging pounding uncomfortable chilled fatigued dry lousy dizzy hyper frozen sweat soft rough sharp flabby sluggish unalert healthy brightness hairy satisfied discomfort.

Feelings
unhappy glad mad sad excited angry moody happy energetic uncomfortable helpless restless awed nervous joy miserable hopeless confined disappointment jubilant edgy apprehensive wanting loving self-confident bored wide-awake content confused impatient sarcastic tired sorrow glad high stoned lonely depressed upset hostile jealous foreign boxed-in kind alienated glowing cherry suicidal violent frightened resentful ambitious responsible discouraged content surprised morose uneasy relaxed uptight worried anxious

confused undecided fearful afraid confident unsure jovial rejected furious rejuvenated revived indifferent passive motivated curious carefree lost alive spacey unwanted forgiving merciful good outspoken stupid dumb bad cocky comfortable pressured embarrassed ashamed loved respected creative estatic mellow at-peace relieved scared frightened friendly distressed put-out honoured introverted outgoing quick unaccomplished pensive agitated despair power hated terror pleasure pride optimistic puzzled apathetic dissatisfied unfulfilled empty complete hateful concerned disheartened peeved drunk.

Note the clear difference in the colour, or feel, of these two sets of words. Having established this distinction, let us concentrate on feelings. Is there any one feeling we all desire to have, the need for which may therefore be said to constitute the fundamental and universal human need?

Traditional philosophy says yes and selects happiness. Everyone wants to be happy, but there's something interesting about the way people describe happiness. They say something like, 'It means everything is going well, not a care in the world.' In other words we tend to conceive of happiness as the absence of what threatens it, as the suspension of snags. Can we think of a state of feeling which would not depend on the absence of unpleasant things but would sustain us even in adverse circumstances? That would be the feeling we all desire to have, for life is chock-full of snags and accidents, as we know all too well. That feeling is, I think, the feeling that whatever happens to me I am significant, I have worth, value, I *am* someone.

We are not so conscious of this need to feel significant as we are of the need to be happy, but it is the real drive, what makes you you. A person's life may become so wretched that he almost forgets the desire to be happy, but he cannot stop wanting to have some value in his own eyes.

The traditional idea that happiness is the universal need is too vague. It fails to touch the nerve of human experience, which is the need to feel that I am someone, that I am not nothing, not worthless. That word 'nerve' is appropriate. Often the need to feel significant is like the nerve of a tooth, only felt when it is not operating well. What hurts in people is often closest to their essential concern. This song in the film *Nashville*

6

It don't worry me,
It don't worry me,
You may say that I ain't free,
But it don't worry me.

is a parody of happiness as the deadening of the human nerve.

The achievement of Ernest Becker is to have highlighted with painful clarity this essential need of the human being to feel significant, worth-full, worthy, someone. When a being becomes self-aware, as happens when evolution breaks onto the human plateau, it must desire significance for itself.

The instinct for survival, which we share with all living things, takes with us the form of feeling worthy to survive. The survival-instinct, become human, is the sense of personal worth. 'Here I am' means just that: here *I* am, and you shall not ignore me. This is brought out by Becker's analysis of the feeling of the soldier in battle that no bullet will get him. He is too important to vanish. Becker adds: 'All that religious and psychoanalytic genius has to tell us converges on the terror of admitting what one is doing to win his self-esteem.' In other words, I attach far more importance to myself than I dare to admit to you. The whole difficulty about counselling, and the reason why good counsellors are rare, is the difficulty of admitting even to myself, let alone to my counsellor, how important I am in my own eyes. What the counsellee tends to do is to make light of his difficulties once the counsellor begins to come close. 'It's OK really, I'm making a mountain out of a mole-hill, I can get by. I don't really need someone to love me and all that.' This is a cop-out, and very human.

If the need to feel significant is the basic human need, the next task will be to see how it flowers and reveals its full meaning in the growing person.

3. The Search Continued

As we begin to move towards adulthood, across the bridge of adolescence, the need to feel significant shows itself as more than the child's craving for attention. I make the crucial discovery that my need to feel significant gets a far fuller, more intense satisfaction when I feel a new attraction for another person. The person who is beginning to be in love has a more intense feeling of personal worth, of status, of really being someone, than ever before. The next discovery is that this new feeling of being attracted, and of being in consequence more worthwhile to myself, contains the intense desire that the other person have an attraction towards me. Should this turn out to be the case, my need to feel significant will receive a further satisfaction: the most intense and delicious satisfaction we ever experience. So we can trace the need to feel significant through three stages of satisfaction:

1. the infant's pleasure at being recognized;
2. the youthful pleasure at being in love;
3. the youthful pleasure in knowing that the beloved is attracted.

With each phase, the basic need reaches a new plateau of fulfilment.

The more a need is fulfilled, the more I know what that need is. The wonderful feeling of the lover, of having got what he always wanted without knowing it, bears this out. But doesn't this contradict my earlier observation that we only experience our need to feel significant when it is not being met: the comparison of the conscious nerve in the aching tooth? I would reply by making a distinction. The presence, the fact, of a need is known by its non-fulfilment; the full meaning of a need is known only in its fulfilment. Maslow makes a very serious mistake when he says that a need once satisfied ceases to be conscious. The need to feel significant, which makes the neglected kid bawl at the corner of the playpen, only reveals where it is going when the eyes of the beloved light up for the lover.

Now comes the last stage in the argument. The eyes of the beloved light up because she is happy, feels more value in her *own* life. The momentous conclusion is that the need which sets the kid bawling will find its final fulfilment in being the cause of happiness, of excitement, of fulfilment, in *another*. In other words, the elemental thrust of life in the human being, the need to feel significant, the essential appetite of self-aware being, finds its full meaning and satisfaction as an act of love which creates happiness in another.

It follows that any philosophy which makes an ultimate opposition between personal fulfilment and other-centredness is false. Our personal fulfilment is in the life-enhancement of another. Short of this, we are not fulfilled.

This has an important implication for the nature of growing up. We should not regard growing up as simply changing, nor as adding new things, like building a house brick by brick. We should regard growing up as entering ever more fully into a destiny which is given at the beginning. It is the progressive clarification of a goal. The need which occurs with the advent of adolescence is not new, but is a further clarification of the original need. The passionate, all-mastering zest to be and to know that I am is not succeeded by the need to feel that I am significantly for another. It reveals its full meaning in that need. In a similar and more easily graspable way, the pleasure in an erection which is felt in infancy only reveals its meaning, only comes into its own, in the attraction felt towards another. We don't add attraction to genital stimulation: the brick-by-brick model. In the same way, we do not add the need to be significantly for another to the need to feel our own worth. Philosophers have coined a word for this exciting idea that a need moves gradually towards a consummation which the person could not foresee but which, when it is realized, reveals the meaning of the need. They call it intentionality. The intentionality of the primal zest to feel myself alive is to enhance with itself the zest for life in another. It is no mere pious or improving cliché that we are, in our most intimate feeling of ourselves, given to each other: that to be consciously alive is to be a gift: that what I most deeply feel myself to be is a gift which enriches another. Thus we arrive at a definition of the essential human need as that need clarifies itself in the growing person. It is the need *to be myself for another.*

As this notion will be central to the book, it will be well to consolidate it at this stage. To this end, a word about definitions. A good definition has two qualities: it must be as brief as possible, having no superfluous words; and it must embrace everything essential to the thing defined. This definition is certainly brief, but doesn't it leave out something essential, namely that for the need to be satisfied I have to be attracted to the other person? It does not suffice that I am there for the other person, that I enhance her life. In fact the definition includes this element. To 'be myself' in a relationship is to be fulfilled, to feel all my being with joy. In the situation we are considering, I am in the presence of another person. To feel happy and fulfilled in the presence of a person is to feel love for that person.

We might attack the definition from the other end and say: 'I might feel all of myself in her presence, I might feel given to her, and she be looking for a way out. So the definition does not comprise her being attracted to me, which it must if it's to measure up to our description of the fully articulated human need.' No again; that little word 'for' is the hinge of the definition. 'I am myself for her' means that she is experiencing as 'for her', as life-enhancing, my being. 'For' refers both to my experience and to hers. It says how I feel and how the other feels.

I begin to be myself for another when I feel the strong attraction to a person. I feel more myself than yesterday, and this 'more myself' is pointing in the direction of a special person. I experience the completion of this 'being-myself-for' when I hear from her that she too is drawn. A vital conclusion follows. The need which is the mainspring of the individual only shows its real meaning where two come together in love and thus form the nucleus of the human community.

I have worked this out in terms of sexual love, because it is easier to see there. In non-sexual friendships the process is also operative; we slowly come to be ourselves for our friends. We probably wouldn't put it that way, it's too intense and dramatic; but in the sexual relationship we have to put it that way, we have to ask ourselves these searching questions about the heart. Thus the dynamic of human interrelationship in its sexual form is more perspicuous and so more available for introspection. It's hardly surprising that what creates the family and the ongoing of the human race should be the mirror in which we see what we are all about.

In sum: the universal human need in its fully adult form is the need 'to be myself for another', with the word 'for' referring both to my attraction to the other and to the other's attraction to me. I offer this definition with some confidence. I cannot think of anything less likely to be disputed than the proposition that everyone wants to be attractive to someone whom they find attractive. This wish goes right across the board from Hitler to Jesus. That we all desire to be desired by one we desire is in practice the least contested proposition known to me.

4. The Question to God

Our self-absorption has a deeper root still to be explored. There is something about my self-awareness which no one else can touch or speak to: I am aware that I am, that I might not have been and that I once was not. Why then am I? Why is there anything at all? Why is there this world into which I am woven? Why is there experience? No one can help me as I wrestle with this question. It is *the* question of myself. It is far more than an intellectual question.

The real source of the human being's absorption with himself, of his endless fascination with himself and of his passionate pursuit of meaningful survival is that he does not know where he comes from or whither he is bound. This self-absorption is at root a huge curiosity. He wonders at his being because he wonders that he is at all. Because he can find in himself and in his world no answer to this question, he becomes more and more preoccupied with it. An insatiable curiosity is an endless curiosity.

It is not that we spend long hours sitting in the posture of the naked thinker in Rodin's famous bronze, with puckered brow and chin on fist. That would be ridiculous. This radical uncertainty about the origin of our being is working away on us beneath the ordinarily conscious level. It is driving us to assert our value to ourselves and to the world. Our contemporary culture, however, makes it very difficult for us to contact this radical insecurity in ourselves. Technology secures us against many of the natural disasters which reminded our ancestors of the dependence of human life on a reality beyond us. But the anxiety is still there.

Eric Voegelin finds human cultural history poised between the sense of an unknown beginning and an unknown end.[1] For him, man is essentially in a 'between' state. Hence every known culture

---

[1] *Order and History*, 4 vols. (Baton Rouge: Louisiana State University Press, 1956–1975).

has abounded in stories, myths, about our origin and our destiny, which are just as much a preoccupation as food, clothing and shelter.

Corroborating this, Becker's central thesis is not simply that we are absorbed with ourselves, but that this self-absorption is the continued and never-successful attempt to deal with the unknownness of our origin by pretending to ourselves that we are of our own making. The 'denial of death' is the denial of our dependence on a mystery which wholly exceeds our grasp. The intensity and universality of the attempted denial is the measure of our basic insecurity.

Now I want to make a bold suggestion. If our self-absorption and passionate pursuit of meaningfulness are at root our inner dialogue with our unknown origin; and if our experience with each other shows that self-absorption finds its meaning and release in knowing that I am significant for someone else; might it not be that my self-absorption is ultimately to find its meaning and release *in knowing that I am significant for the unknown reality that is my origin?* In other words the human being, in all his self-fascination, in all his posturing, in all his 'look-at-me', might be, without realizing it, behaving towards the ultimate mystery in the way a man behaves when he is in love, in the absurd way the Hunchback of Notre Dame behaves when he rings all the bells, realizing he is in love with the beautiful lady.

Sometimes a person who really turns you on starts you feeling so good about yourself that you start showing off, talking too much and making a fool of yourself. Perhaps our constitution in being near an unknown reality which wholly exceeds our grasp is in reality a turn-on whose consummation would come if we could somehow know that we are indeed significant in its, in his, or her, 'eyes'. Perhaps the whole vast panoply of human culture and performance is an act of worship which never quite gets off the ground. If our human self-absorption is at root our dialogue with our unknown origin, is it not the self-absorption of the lover awaiting the news that the other is interested?

Certainly all religions try to make us believe this. Religion presupposes, and purports to satisfy, a need to know that we are loved by the mystery with which we are in any case desperately concerned. Yet in all religiousness there lurks the suspicion that we invented the story that God loves us. The unique thing about the

13

Christian belief in God's love is that it arose only after the execution of Jesus had produced in his followers a total disillusionment with all religion. The risen Jesus came to them from beyond the whole complex human apparatus of make-believe. This idea must await explanation at the end of the book.

In religion there lurks the fear that we invented the story of God's love. The modern psyche, deprived of the ancient stories and possessed only of the scientific accounts, is in a much worse case than the religious person who fears he *may* be the source of the story. The scientific explanation doesn't even pretend to be a revelation. It is only something thought up, and as such is not strong enough to minister to our metaphysical insecurity.

A movie like *Close Encounters of the Third Kind* is evidence of the terrible loneliness created by the psychic vacuum: the desire to believe that, in the limitless galactic wastes, we are not alone. For all its technological splendour, the huge visiting space ship is meeting much more primitive and eternal needs in the audience. Again, the beautiful songs of the hump-backed whale were recently sent, on a recording, into deep space. They were part of the information placed in a space capsule destined to journey for 1.2 billion years on the off-chance of meeting someone. Bleak!

What we have done so far in this chapter is to show that the need 'to be myself for another' is, in its deepest form, a religious need. One of the most serious mistakes made in this affair of God, religious people often being the worst offenders, is to think that our relationship with God does not exist until we believe, or pray, or connect with God in some conscious way. In reality, before we do any of this, and whether we do it or not, we exist in what might be called a psychic-organic relationship with God. I use this name simply as a label for that deep, generally unrecognized anxiety about where we come from and where we are going. Whether we call that anxiety an unease with createdness, as Becker does, or an anxious curiosity about the beginning and end, as Voegelin does, or as a flight from the Hound of Heaven, as the poet Francis Thompson does, it's certainly a *relationship* with God, and a very gutsy one.

To that anxiety religion speaks. To that anxiety the life of Jesus gets through in a unique way. This anxiety asks: Does the ultimate mystery, which causes me to be this anxious, self-absorbed, posturing creature, care about me? I am suggesting that this anxiety

14

might be compared to that of the lover who is wondering anxiously how the beloved feels. The comparison may seem far-fetched, but as the question 'how does *she* feel?' is the most anxious and life-investing question we ever ask, it seems likely that we are asking it also at the frontiers of our existence.

What is the religious question? Why do we want to know about God? It is the question 'Are we significant in God's eyes?', but this needs an edge. I suggest: 'Do our love-affairs have ultimate significance?' That sounds romantic: marriages made in heaven and all that. I don't mean it that way, but rather: 'Are we who have love-affairs ultimately significant?' Is there an ultimate reality which has everything to do with who we find ourselves to be as we strive to live to the full?

We taste life. We test it. We risk it. We invest more and more of ourselves in it. Of all this investment and attendant risk, the love-affair is at least the privileged metaphor. Is it like that, in the end? Is the universe made that way, or is this thing we humans chase just the extraordinary human side-step from the way of the universe? The only serious form of the religious question today is: Is human self-awareness, when it finds its fulfilment in love, resonating, albeit faintly, with an origin that 'behaves', infinitely and all-constitutingly, as love behaves? Is the question 'Am I significant?' solicited from me by the lover for me to address an answer to him or her in the way that only lovers talk, questioning what lovers know because it is too good not to be true?

Shortly before his religious conversion Eliot phrased this, the real religious question, with the poignant possibility of disappointment:

> Is it like this
> In death's other Kingdom
> Waking alone
> At the hour when we are
> Trembling with tenderness, lips that would kiss
> Form prayers to broken stone.

The question 'Are we significant to God?' is the religious question. It always was, and it always will be; but for this question to come from us with the appropriate urgency, it has to be asked the way a lover questions the beloved. We know too much about ourselves, we have experienced too much, not to be enormously tempted by the theory of the human side-step. Only a God who negates for us the idea of the human side-step is believable. The only God who will do this is he whose love is sought by us in the way that we ask of the beloved: 'Do you love me?' The question to the beloved is *the* human question. It brings to a head human self-awareness. For human self-awareness to have ultimate significance is, equivalently, for its central question to probe an ultimate beloved.

At this stage I am not asking the reader to believe in such a beloved. I am only asking him or her to consider whether the whole gamut of human experience, organized round the central thrust 'to be myself for another', might be understood as having, for its centre, that question to the ultimate which men and women know, in their human relationships, so terribly well.

Another way of getting at the real religious question is to ask: Does 'Who am I?' turn into 'Why am I?', a question meaningfully asked only of the cause of my existence? Does self-awareness as such, at its most vital, question the cause of existence with the only serious question it knows, the question one asks of the beloved when all one's meaningful existence is at stake?

If God is, he made us. But the idea of myself as of another's making is so total, so all-embracing, that it as-it-were swamps me. It seems to take up the story at another level altogether than the level I'm on when I speak of 'being myself for another'. Clay in the hands of the potter is all very well, but you cannot go on to say that the whole point about this clay is in the initiatives it takes, in the striving to have and give meaning, and that this is the clay's way to the Potter! This problem indicates vividly that the religious question nowadays has to conceive of the making, constitutive nature of God as some unimaginable, possible, bliss-giving 'Yes' to a question which the self-aware person increasingly learns himself to be. The religious question today is, quite simply, mystical. Religion as a decency is out. It is either transforming or it is nothing. It is a question of the availability or non-availability of a permanently transformed existence.

Never before have we had to seek God with what is so intimately ourselves, to use as probe our very selves. It is fascinating that while the notion of God as maker seems to swamp the quest for meaning at the ultimate level, it is rather congenial when we feel

16

disappointed or disaffected with life. At those times we think of ourselves not as unfolding miracle but as sheer fact and refer the whole thing, without difficulty or enthusiasm, to the factor. It is an eloquent proof of the inadequacy of the potter metaphor that it offers itself when our spirituality is at its slackest. To look ahead for a moment, we shall see, when we come to consider guilt, that the latter consists precisely in this servile 'Well, you made me' attitude to God. To look still further ahead, to seek to articulate the human hunger for God in a way which depends solely on the sense of life as unfolding miracle and not at all on the self as sheer fact, is to grope towards that miracle of human psychology, the self-awareness of Jesus.

The decade of the 1970s has been called the me-generation. Religious critics of this generation are saying: ' "Who am I?" is the selfish question. It's time to ask "Why am I?" ' This critique easily misses the whole point: that the question 'Who am I?' itself breaks into the question 'Why am I?', which is thus asked with a mystical intensity never known before. The critics may well be reverting to the 'swamping' form of the God-question, thus missing that edge of meaning and evangel God is beginning to have at this troubled turn of time. That edge appears when a new and daring introspection finds, at the heart of the whole human life-thrust, an investment of feeling in the cause of our existence comparable only to the terrible investment we make in an unforgettable face.

If God is, he is our maker; but the notion of 'our maker' is a kind of metaphysical blank, to be filled in with each increment in self-awareness as human culture pursues its wayward and sporadic course.

There is no suggestion here that the notion of God as maker be superseded or that God be regarded as a force which 'finds expression' in human beings. Nor is there any place in my thought for the God of process philosophy and theology, who changes as we develop. The God whose act of creation has been well described as a loving self-limitation, and who dies that we might live to him, is a profound mystery which may not be understood in terms of our concept of process and change. Process theology is anthropomorphism without its primitive beauty. It has always evoked for me the colour of grey. The dominion of God is, in my conception, absolute; but it is the dominion of the beloved. It is that dominion over us which we acknowledge in part wherever our unfolding sense of ourselves is invested. It is that dominion become total when, through a blessed and honest simplification of ourselves, we confess that our self-making is a swift and wild river of desire which runs out to the unknown and yearns to hear from that mysterious beloved. The author of *The Cloud of Unknowing,* who speaks of a darting of love into the Cloud, is describing the faithful appropriation of that river of desire.

5. A Startling Conclusion

The more we look at the religious question this way, the more an astonishing conclusion emerges: only on this supposition can there be God at all. To believe that God is, is to believe that my experience of not being my own maker finds its organizing centre in a looking to another for meaning; and of this looking the look of Dante to Beatrice is the paradigm. Not to believe that God is, is to believe that this experience of dependence has no such core, but is simply the sense of being a product of parents, of the cosmic process, of whatever. In other words, the sense of dependence and the hunger for meaning have not, in the unbeliever, come together.

'That without which I would not be' could be the evolutionary process, or the strategic dropping of my mother's handkerchief, presuming the normal mating pattern of that culture was followed. 'That without which I would not be' has the allure of God only when sensed by the questing heart which quickens to the presence of a beloved and seeks from her the word of life, the permission to live.

It is with the heart that God is sought. It is for the heart that God is God. It is through an ultimate trusting of his heart that a man finds God. This is why God says: 'I will be to him a Father and he will be to me a son.' It is with something akin to God, it is with a divine sonship of the heart which is the inerrant pilot at the core of our being, that God is sought and his word prized.

'Man does not live by bread alone, but by every word that comes from the mouth of God.' Our dependence by itself, our physical dependence on the universe, is not our way into life until it reveals itself as the dependence for meaning. There is my utter dependence on that which is not I; there is my hunger for meaning; these two. Ernest Becker recovered these two key realities of our existence, saw that they were connected, but never saw the connection. He thought we pursued meaning by suppressing our sense of dependence. Blinded by the rationalism of our culture, he never saw through to the devastating simplicity which unites the sense of dependence with the desire for meaning: they come together as the *dependence for meaning:* that dependence of which we learn when we fall in love, experience the need to hear, and learn all the other ways of humility.

Luther said: 'God is that in which the heart of a man rests. If the resting is right the God is right. If the resting is wrong the God is wrong.' A brilliant saying, in search of an answer to the question: 'What is a right resting?' The answer is: when the heart which finds meaning to rest in is the heart which humbly knows man's total dependence in this world. The heart is the guide when the heart is giving its own meaning to the otherwise heartless fact that I depend totally on that which is not I.

Is not this intensely interpersonal understanding of God individualistic? Quite the reverse. It has me seeking and sensing God with that in me which looks to others to grow with, to be with, to build with. In contrast, a confused theism whose God is really a warmed-up cosmic force is an umbrella of impersonality under which every kind of individualism can thrive. The Bible says that what is heard 'in the chambers' is to be 'cried from the housetops'.

A German mystic, Angelus Silesius, once said: 'If God ceased to think of me he would cease to exist.' This is not egoism, but an unusually clear statement of what it means to be God, expressing the soul's native sense for the beloved who calls the soul by name. 'God loved us first', says John. That first loving is God's making love our climate, in which we find ourselves, come to ourselves, and then obscurely sense the infinite unknown as the soul's beloved. Augustine said '*Noverim me, noverim te*': 'Let me know myself; let me know you.' These knowings are indivisible.

Without the heart, the sense of total dependence is annihilating. Yet when they come together, the heart finds in the sense of total dependence a cause for love more radical than we ever know between persons. I depend on a special person for a new leap in life, not for life itself. My central quest for meaning, the most intimately promising grail-quest of the heart, looks to that without which I would not be at all and finds there the theme of the greatest love. The heart alone mines the precious stone of our total physical contingency and polishes it to refract the light of all being.

From this burning centre of all humanness we have drifted into an endlessly prosecuted rationalism on the one hand and into a blind, privatized affectivity on the other. So deep and habitual is the split between mind and heart that one despairs of mending it intelligibly. But it is God who mends the split, by teaching us the blazing, humbling truth: for all the meanings we find and with which we fill our libraries and lecture halls, we are dependent for meaning as the lover depends on the word of the beloved that he is loved. It is this central communication, this permission to have ultimate meaning, which is received graciously from God, which shows us that the mind and the heart are one.

6. Are We Naturally in Love with God?

The central human need, as we have seen, finds its full satisfaction when I know that the other is attracted to me. This is the second 'quantum leap of the heart', which everyone craves.

I now propose that in a religious conversion the person experiences, with God, the second quantum leap. He becomes totally convinced that the God with whom he is already in love is in love with him: that the God he already finds significant finds him significant.

This is ridiculous, I hope you are saying. The whole point of a religious conversion is that before it happens the person does *not* care about God. That's what a religious conversion is: falling in love with God. It's the first quantum leap, not the second. To sustain my thesis, I have to show that the human person, in his or her pre-religious phase, is 'in love with God'.

We hold onto nothing so tenaciously as that which comes to us by luck. Life has come to us by luck, so it is amazingly precious to us. Our self-fascination reaches out, gropingly, towards whatever it might be that contains the secret of our existing. At this stage I am addressing a question to this other reality: 'Everything tells me I am important, yet I don't know why I exist. I shall always have a sneaking suspicion I am deceiving myself about my importance unless you tell me that I am important to you. Do I count in your eyes?'

For a person to receive the answer, 'Yes, you are precious in my eyes, I made you out of love' would surely be the second quantum leap. Our pre-religious existence, we have seen, is a passionate concern, grounded in self-absorption, with the mystery of our origin. This is our first quantum leap in relation to the mystery.

We are born and bred into a race which is 'in love with God', stirred with a sense of preciousness that gropes towards mystery. We are born and bred into the first quantum leap in relation to the purpose of our existence. All the great religions try to bring us into the second quantum leap: the conviction that we are significant to him who is totally significant to us because he is our reason for existing.

That person with whom I am becoming fascinated is not my reason for existing; there is not *that* cause for fascination. How much more intensely does the ultimate mystery of our being in this world lay hold of the heart! Is not this central affair we have with the ultimate mystery the thing which gives shape to all our relationships? The reason why I feel a growth in my worth when I know I am significant to a significant other is that I am psychically wedded, of my very nature, to the significant other that gives me my being. Other-grounded, we are other-oriented.

7. The Idea of a Natural Love Affair with God

In exploring our human relationships we simply took as fact our need to feel significant. The question of God arises when we go beyond seeing this need as fact and ask why we have it, where it comes from. The source of that fascination of man with himself which shapes all he does and makes is that he does not know whence he comes, why he is, whither he is bound. Why should this ignorance be the source of self-fascination? This is a difficult question.

To approach an answer, we have to get as clear an idea as possible of this ignorance. How does it really feel not to know why I exist? That's quite a question. It is the search for a feeling that is deeply buried, overlaid by all our inbred systems for coping with the world we have to live in.

I am curious about why I exist. But wait a minute! Can I say that? I am talking about me, about this self for whom I so much care and have to care, the self that is desperately self-preserving. Can I, referring to something as precious as me, use a detached word like 'curiosity' to describe how I feel about my unknown origin and purpose and destiny?

Suppose you are awoken at 2.00 A.M. to find the light on and a squad of menacing, uniformed men around your bed. You are told to get dressed, then you are handcuffed, bundled into a car, transferred to a train with boarded windows with a crowd of other prisoners unknown to you. As the train moves off into the night, would you describe yourself as 'curious' as to what is afoot? Or consider the terrifying experience of the Marquette student in the film *Midnight Express*; or the experience of the tiny Jewish child packed into a crowded cattle-truck with no one he knew.

Whether or not these nightmare experiences are a parable of modern man uprooted from religious tradition and lost in an alien universe, my purpose here is simply to get us thinking about how each of us would feel, if really exposed to the feeling of not knowing why he exists. If ignorance about what is happening to me in a particular incident is terrifying, how much more terrifying must be such ignorance when it concerns not merely my fate in this instance, but my very existence. Of course we don't feel this terror—and thank God we don't! But I think it must be present. Our deep, unnoticed feelings are what really influence our behaviour.

When awoken in the night and carried off, I am more than usually aware of myself and how dear my life is to me; this self-preoccupation is centred on not knowing what is going on. The self-awareness is intensified by the ignorance. Would not the deeper ignorance we have as to our very being be the source of an even more intense self-awareness? I am suggesting that the passionate self-absorption which characterizes the whole human race is, at root, this more intense self-absorption. The absolute conviction we have that we matter is grounded in concern about our origin and destiny. In other words, the conviction that we matter is really a question addressed to the unknown origin and shaper of our being.

This question concerns us and our well-being more intimately than any other. It is therefore a most passionate question, a question on which our very life depends. In this 'question to the unknown other' we find all the elements of the question to the beloved: the feeling that my life is at stake and the sense of the other as holding all the cards. Could it be that the question to the unknown other is the supreme instance of that 'question to the beloved' on which our most significant interpersonal life hinges? Could it be that the 'supreme instance' is what makes us other-directed beings?

This would mean that God, the ultimate mystery, is the 'beloved' of man before ever religion comes to him. This may seem far-fetched; but consider what people have done when they have thrown off the Church, as happened when Marxism and similar movements were born. They thought they were simply freeing themselves to be themselves without priests to tell them what they must do. At this greater distance of time, we can see that in reality they were making for themselves an 'other' which would make their lives significant, whether they called it Progress, or History, or Manifest Destiny, or The Party, or the Millennium. They were arranging to be loved and built up. They sought from some other the reassuring word: 'Yes, your life is valuable to me.' They sought

25

this word in these ways because they no longer heard it from the Church.

We are much more emotionally involved with God, or at least with the question of God, than we like to think or to admit. This emotional involvement with God is the key to our self-understanding and to the understanding of religion. It is pre-religious. Religion is the believed-in answer of the unknown other, to the question: 'Am I valuable in your eyes?' Unless we can come to understand the question as our question and the most human thing about us, we shall never understand the religious answer as the fulfilment of our whole desire for meaning. The greatest need in theology today is to discover and to name this pre-religious emotional involvement with God.

In sum: three theses

Thesis 1
There is an erotic dependence of the human being on the ultimate constitutive mystery that is pre-religious, universal, in the radical sense conscious, and shaping of all human life and culture.

Thesis 2
The passionate intensity of man's self-absorption is due precisely to his not containing within himself the reason, purpose or meaning of his existence. It is an other-questioning self-absorption.

Thesis 3
This expands thesis 1. All the person's relationships are shaped by this primordial dynamic of the self-absorbed being towards the other. Self-absorption, the absolute conviction of my significance, looks to the mystery that is other for the enjoyment of this significance and therefore looks to the 'significant other' person for that enjoyment in the human community.

8. Laying Bare Our Logic

Step 1
The question 'Why am I?' is not an intellectual or a curiosity question but a feeling, passionate one, involving me at the roots of my being.

Step 2
Feeling questions, as opposed to intellectual questions, are addressed to an other. Things you need to know you ask about.

Step 3
Therefore the question 'Why am I?' is addressed to an other.

Step 4
The only 'other' who could answer it would be the ultimate reality that constitutes all things in being, if there is such an ultimate reality.

Step 5
Therefore the question 'Why am I?' is addressed to this ultimate reality.

Step 6
But the question 'Why am I?', addressed to the ultimate reality, is the question 'What is my significance in your eyes?', which contains the question 'Am I significant in your eyes?'

27

Step 7

But the question 'Am I significant in your eyes?' is the question to the beloved.

Step 8

Therefore the ultimate reality is the beloved.

In short:

The most life-laden question we know is, in the depths of our being, addressed to Life Itself.

This is not a proof for God's existence. It is a proof that human beings are, pre-religiously and universally, emotionally involved in the question of God.

9. Alternative Form of the Argument

This argument from the 'question to the Beloved' to the 'question to God' can be thus explained:

1. We are always asking other people who we are. The very notion of 'my identity' appeals to another, for my identity is my unique value, to which I cannot attain if I ignore the valuer. Significant existence, which is the one thing a person must have to feel he is a person, depends upon appreciation. It is therefore of others, as potential appreciators, that we ask 'Who am I?'

2. Once the central human desire and need is properly understood as the need to be myself for another, the question 'Who am I?' is seen to be an other-directed question, which holds pent-up the love energy in whose release alone I experience full personhood. The question 'Who am I?' presses on to the question 'Why am I?', giving the latter its passionate character. 'Who am I?' means, ultimately, 'Who am I to you?'

3. Of most people I ask this question in vain. In fact I hardly ask it. The child is still asking it of everyone. Its infirm little ego seeks on all sides support for the enormous claim man makes for himself, to have a purpose in this vast, indifferent world.

4. Of the significant other, I ask this question with urgency and some appropriateness. Someone to whom I am important will know why I exist: to be the person I am for her. She doesn't really know why I exist, of course, but she is much closer to being able to answer my question 'Why am I?' than is the person I meet in the street.

5. I ask the question 'Why am I?' with the greatest urgency of the cause of my being. For the urgency, the hopefulness, with which a question is asked, depends on the need for an answer and on the capacity of the questioned one to answer. This capacity is simply and totally present in God.

29

The argument, in sum, is that the question 'Why am I?' is of its nature the question to the beloved, to the significant other; and that since this question is addressed most appropriately to God, God is the beloved, the significant other, of the soul.

10. The Anomaly of our God-Connectedness

The thing I most want to know is this: what I am worth, what meaning I have. Where I am most ignorant about this, there I most need to know. I am most ignorant about my worth in relation to the ultimate purpose of my existence on this planet. Therefore I need above all to know whether I have meaning for the power that puts me in existence. But the only context in which I vividly and painfully experience the desire to know my worth is the context of human relations; even though my ignorance, my need to know, is far greater in the context of my ultimate purpose. Hence a curious imbalance: where my need to know my worth is most felt, it is less great; and where it is greatest it is least felt. Thus one reason why people don't readily become conscious of their need to hear from God is that they don't see the connection between needing to hear from God and needing to hear from the girl- or boy-friend. The place of maximum ignorance needs to coincide with the experience of the desire to know. People need their greatest need to become their greatest want.

The fully developed religious personality is one for which this greatest need has become the greatest want.

11. Some Implications of the Pre-religious Love Affair With God

Underlying my self-feeling is a passionate investment in the unknown that knows me. This invests certain people I meet with an exciting, inviting quality. Everyone finds certain people exciting and inviting: it's their invitation into life and growth. These 'significant others' are touched, for me, with the primordial allure of *the* other who holds the secret of my existence.

To consolidate this idea, I shall now do three things. First, I shall try to suggest why it is true. Second, I shall explain where it fits and where it does not fit into Becker's schema. Third, I shall outline some of its consequences.

First, is it true? Supposing you understood yourself perfectly. Everything you felt, you understood why. Every person you felt drawn to, you knew exactly what in you was being triggered by what in them. Every dream checked out completely: you could 'read' every figure in the dream. Every experience checked out completely. You would be totally transparent to yourself. How would that be? It would very soon be boring. More than that, your life would no longer be your life. It would be more like your car or your radio. You would no longer be of any interest to yourself. In other words the essence of you would have dropped out. The element of mystery in ourselves is the spice of life. On the other hand, simply not knowing is not enough. Life would also be boring if some other people and opportunities did not seem to offer a clue to who you are. Life is a subtle blending of self-ignorance with looking to significant others. This blend has its foundation in the feeling that a person has of himself in 'dialogue' with the 'other' that perhaps knows all. This condition is what I call the pre-religious hunger for God's acceptance.

Second: in relation to Becker. Becker has the two main elements of the total picture: the sense of personal uniqueness and the sense

of total dependence on a total mystery. But he sees the first as absolutely against the second. I build myself, I get my act together, I
develop my character in spite of the haunting knowledge that I
came out of an egg just like other animals do. My character is a
'lie', for it is the result of systematically denying my creaturehood. Well-integrated people are those who are best at living this
lie, who are most comfortable with it. The schizophrenic is helpless
because he is bombarded simultaneously with the demands of
civilized living (the lie) and the onrush of darkness and mystery
which surrounds the self. He can't hold the lie amidst the storm.

We must not be in too much of a hurry to say that this is obviously false. A tremendous proportion of people's lives consists in
the denial of creaturehood. The big entrepreneur who builds an
empire at the cost of all his natural feelings of tenderness and bewilderment would be an example. Much of your life and mine is
describable in these terms.

The crucial question is: What am I doing when I deny my creaturehood? I am dodging my relationship with the all-embracing
other. This relationship is the deepest thing about me. It makes me
who I am. Only by slowly recognizing it and accepting it will I
come into spiritual and psychic health. My relationship with the
all-embracing other is not the confrontation with a sheer threat
which would annihilate my personhood. It is the secret of precisely
that sense of my worth which drives me forward and tempts me to
forget my ultimate moorings in the mystery that gives me being.

Becker never asked about the positive, life-enhancing possibilities which lurk for us in the unknown other. He only saw the negative, threatening possibilities. Nowhere is Becker able to describe,
in concrete terms, the remedy for the evil he cogently describes.

The positive element in our dialogue with the unknown other is
woven into all our ordinary experience, because this dialogue, not
our running-away, gives the essential zest to our life. The other is
the beloved. Anyone who has experienced a powerful love affair
knows that one can be angry with the beloved, even hate her, avoid
her, lie to her, rage at her—which is not a bad description of our
relationship with God. The reason why the Psalms have always
stood out as the best prayer-models is that they reflect all these
moods.

As a way of unifying what Becker sees as divided, we need to see
our dialogue with 'the unknown that knows me' as the source of

our conviction of personal uniqueness and worth. Here's an allegory that might help. Suppose we're discussing John, who is showing odd behaviour towards a girl called Mary, whom he sees at
parties from time to time. In the allegory Mary represents the unknown, our mystery, our mortality. John says vicious things about
her sometimes. He has been known to get up and leave the moment she comes into the room. She seems to be a threat to him.
What's the diagnosis? Becker's diagnosis would be: 'Mary is a
threat to John; she totally undermines, he thinks, his personality;
yet John cannot altogether keep out of her way.' The beyond-
Becker diagnosis would be: 'John is in love with Mary and is fighting against this.'

To ignore Becker is to ignore the human problem. The negative
elements in our positive relationship with the all-embracing other
are many and various but it is a question of seeing these in the
fuller context suggested by the 'John is in love with Mary' allegory.
That fuller context is an erotic (-desire-shaped) dependence on the
unknown other who knows us, an erotic dependence which is pre-
religious, universal, conscious at the deepest level, and shaping of
all we think and do.

At the end of his famous hymn to Love (1 Cor. 13) St Paul gives
a brilliant description of the final religious consummation as fulfilling all the potential in the pre-religious God-hunger: 'Now I
know in part. Then I shall know even as I am known.' As this describes the final vision, The Heavenly Country, this should strictly
be called 'post-religious' rather than 'religious'.

Third, here are five consequences of this new idea:

1. Religious conversion, which is the experiencing by a person
of the certainty that God loves him, is seen not as starting the person's relationship with God but as advancing it to the point of that
release of the human eros for which the whole being of a person
craves: the release through knowing that the person I love loves
me—that release, in this case, taking place at the centre of my
being, where the need to be significant to the significant other is
originally constituted. Only if man is in his self-awareness God-
questioning as the lover questions the beloved can religious conversion, the received answer of the beloved, be the radical fulfilment of man, the release of all his energies. Religion as fulfilment
depends on the pre-religiousness of the human being's affair with
God. God's word of love to man is the answer to the question that

man *is* to God. Man is the question to the ultimate constitutive mystery, 'Am I valuable in your eyes?' Everything he does and makes, well and ill, betokens that fact. If we do not find the question to God throughout the whole length and breadth and depth of human experience, we shall never hear the word of God as the word of life: that is, as indeed the word of God.

2. The widespread ineffectiveness of organized religion today is due to its failure to speak to the pre-religious God-awareness. Organized religion associates the idea of God so exclusively with the explicitly religious phase in the human God-adventure that it does not help people to recognize the reality of God in their experience of themselves and their lives. It is on this primordial reality of God in human life that the religious recognition of God is built. Thus in this bad deal, both the non-religious and the religious suffer: the non-religious suffer the frustration of their deepest possibilities for self-understanding, which are to do with their pre-religious dialogue with mystery; the religious people have a shallow idea of God, which is tied up with the name of God and has no roots in their deeper and universal human experience. This situation has provoked the comment: 'If there is a God, it is the believers who will get the surprise.'

3. Christian theology over the last century or so has been swinging between two extremes, represented respectively by Schleiermacher, the great theologian of human religious aspiration, and Barth, the great theologian of God's love as a reality that comes to us from beyond. From the standpoint of a concept of pre-religious God-desire, this opposition is seen to be false. The power and the glory of the gospel, as the proclamation that God loved us before we loved him, consists precisely in liberating our pre-religious God-hunger. The gospel is good news because it is the 'Yes' of the beloved.

4. A Swedish theologian named Anders Nygren wrote a very influential book called *Agape and Eros*.[2] His idea is that the pure gospel idea of divine love or *Agape* is of a love that comes to us from beyond ourselves, to which our only response can be faith, not human love. According to him all the writings of the Christian mystics about our love for God are a corruption of this tradition. Again, the false opposition between man's pre-religious yearning

[2] *Agape and Eros* (New York: Harper and Row, 1969).

for God and God's gospel love for man which in fact fulfils it. Faith is indeed the way we receive the message of God's love, but the message is essentially the invitation to all the love energy in man to become actual. Faith is hearing the answer of the beloved, hearing the good news that changes one's whole life.

5. The idea makes possible a more radical understanding of what was happening at the French Revolution and in all the 'rights of man' movements which constitute the modern age. The initiators of these movements thought they were getting free of the God-relationship, which they identified with the Church and the *ancien régime*. Actually they were only changing its content, directing it to a seemingly more man-favouring God called Enlightenment or Progress or History or the Millennium or Manifest Destiny. The spiritual vacuum of our time is due to the collapse of these gods. This diagnosis becomes clear once we understand that the hunger for God's approval is built right into the human heart and cannot be got rid of. The attempt to get rid of it by doing things like closing churches is like thinking that by abolishing the institution of marriage we could stop men and women from expecting fidelity of each other. The response of the Mexican people to the Pope's recent visit is a striking comment on fifty years of systematic attempts to eliminate religion.

12. The Question to God Grounds the Question to the Human Beloved

The strange thing about the question to God is that it seems at first to be markedly less real than the question to the beloved, but on further reflection appears much more real. Of the beloved I ask more life, more meaning, more being in the eyes of another, while of this mysterious deeper other, I am asking whether I have *any* meaning in his/her/its scheme of things. It's not easy to catch yourself asking this question, but I think you do.

We have been comparing what seems less real with what seems more real, but now we say: Isn't it the other way on? The questioning of the human beloved is perhaps powered by and modelled on that questioning of God which is the very heart of a person's life. Is it not because we are God-questioners that we are significant-other questioners? Is it not because we obscurely know that our significant life is in his hands that we experience our life, at significant moments, as held for us by a significant other?

The Mystics are people who become highly developed at this deeper level. They are people for whom, if you like, the quotes we put around the mysterious beloved drop off. When they compare the union of the human spirit with God with the sexual union, which they often do, they talk as though they were really comparing the sexual union with the union they are experiencing.

When we take this bold step of saying 'it's the other way on', we are filling out the description of the pre-religious God-need as 'shaping of all humans do and make'. An understanding of our God-connection as shaping everything in human life would revolutionize our religiousness and its relevance to the world. It would, for instance, illuminate the darkest, most problematic and most emotion-laden area in the contemporary Christian mind, the connection between Christian faith and political involvement. The privatization of religion severs the connection between the religious and the political, and thereafter all attempts by religion to get back into politics are distorted. They are the attempts of an exile to return, whether clandestinely as in the case of Christian human rights movements as we have them, or openly as in those cases where a totalitarian regime is persuaded to co-opt the Church into a restoration of Christian civilization. We have to go to the root of the privatization of religion, which happens because we do not see religion as the recognition of an already existing orientation to the transcendent. This non-recognition is socially and politically ruinous. A telling example is Marxism, whose unavowed hunger for the transcendent turns inwards and devours everything in humanity that opposes it.

It is frequently remarked that 'the language of transcendence became unacceptable in the nineteenth century'. The nineteenth century was the century of the emancipation of thought and culture from the Church, which began with the French Revolution at the close of the preceding century. Early in our century, Freud did the job psychologically. Whereas Darwin had made our spirituality biologically a by-product, and Marx had made it economically an epiphenomenon, Freud clinched the matter by making it psychologically a cover-up. Under the influence of these powerful minds, orientation-to-mystery ceased to be thought of as an integral dimension of human experience. In other words, the pre-religious God-need was dropped from the culture. This meant that people ceased to think of their lives as God-centred except in Church. The Church was the only place left where the 'language of transcendence' was spoken. This meant that the language of transcendence itself changed: it went 'churchy'. The language of transcendence, once it is dropped by the culture, goes pious. It is now practically impossible even to speak about the question as to whether God is, without sounding pious.

We are still in the magnetic field of the nineteenth-century veto on the language of transcendence. Becker is spearheading something new. He has been grabbed by the idea of all human life and culture and history as a kind of wrestle with something bigger than us that prevails through our death. This means he is getting hold of the transcendence dimension again, the larger-than-man dimension in human living. But he is only able to get hold of the negative aspect, the threat, as is to be expected. It is not possible for a powerfully anthropocentric culture like ours to go all the way in one step to a transcendence-centred vision. Becker is half-way out of the womb of the old culture.

13. A Look at the West

'Despite centuries of effort, most if not all Western philosophies fall short of an ethic of love. They invariably make other people into valuable investments which will pay off eventually in the dividends of one's own self-realisation. As one of my favourite teachers, the late Harvard philosopher John Wild, once said, after a lifetime of reading and teaching in the field of ethics, "In fact every influential ethics that has been formulated in our intellectual history is some version of self-realisation!" '

Thus writes the theologian Harvey Cox. If no western philosophies or psychologies have succeeded in centring themselves on love, we have to ask why. It is obvious that we humans are together, indeed a 'togetherness', a society, and that no significant human activity can be described without some reference to this fact. It is also clear that the most achieved togetherness we know is love. So one would expect a philosophy, a systematic account of being human, to find its centre in this most luminous example of human togetherness. Essentially we are together. We make sense when we live together to the fullest extent, that is to say when we live together in love. Philosophy, seeking as it does to make sense of our life, should be attracted to the place where we make most sense, namely in love. Why isn't it?

There seems to be something about love, and that something the essence, which eludes the systematic mind, which slips away like a fish back into its dark habitat. Love means, all at once, self and other. Either the philosopher will concentrate on the 'self' and his potential and then, however altruistically he conceives of the self's highest realization, the other gets left in the shade; or he will concentrate on 'the other' and his demands. In that case, however much the philosopher insists that it is in meeting the true demands of another that I fulfil myself, he never quite succeeds in saying why. Hedonism, ranging from the sensual to the spiritual, and altruism fight over this elusive thing, love, like two dogs over a bone.

A philosophy able to overcome this tendency to break down into either a self-centred or an other-centred system must ask the following question: What is there in a person which, when developed, is manifestly the fulfilment of the self and manifestly the fulfilment of an other person? 'Manifestly', for anyone can *say* that in love I am both fulfilled and fulfilling. Anyone can refer to the undoubted experience of lovers. Our task, however, is to *show* something: to explain how love works, what its structure is.

What is that 'something in a person'? Clearly it is in the order of need or desire. Throughout this book, I have argued that our basic need, felt as an inescapable desire, is to feel uniquely significant. Is this need the 'missing link' between self-fulfilment and other-fulfilment which would make possible a philosophy of love? The very concept of 'feeling significant' appeals to another or to others for its meaning. I may want to feel 'happy', or 'good', or 'high', or 'content', or 'peaceful', or 'secure': these are states of myself, which do not necessarily imply that anyone else comes in on the act. But when I say I want to feel significant, I am talking about a state of myself which looks to others in some way. The need for significance is the need for acceptance. If my need to feel significant is the very condition of my being someone at all, it follows that my essential need requires for its fulfilment some acceptance or at least imagined acceptance by another or others.

Before we start thinking about love, when we are still considering only the self in its basic constitution, we are already thinking, obliquely, about another or others. Significance is significance-for. As I mature, my 'significance for the other' begins to mean all that it says, 'significance *for the other*'. Significance-for-the-other gets as much weight in 'the other' as it initially had in myself. Initially I need, for my psychological survival, to be *significant* for another. As I mature, I need to be significant *for another*. I need to count in another's life, to be the enhancement of another's life.

This need fulfilled is the condition known as love. This condition is manifestly my fulfilment: I am *significant* for the other. This condition is manifestly the fulfilment of another: I am significant *for another*. The 'something' in me whose fulfilment is both my fulfilment and another's is that hunger to be significant which is other-dependent at the start of life and other-fulfilling as we mature.

In other words, the person is, from the beginning and of his or her essence, in a relationship. This relationship reaches its maturity

40

in love. The most radical and shaping desire in a person is a self-other connection whose development is the progressive emergence of the second focus. From being the oblique and me-affirming presence of childhood, the other becomes directly and self-affirmingly present to the maturing self.

The other who comes to me in love is the fleshing-out of the vaguely other who applauded me in childhood. The philosophies have never been centred in love because their creators forgot that first vague presence of the other in the desire of the self to feel significant. They started by conceiving of the self, the individual, without the other. They were therefore never able to get from this initially other-less self to the other without either centring on self, with the other in the shade, or centring on the other with self in the shade. The whole muddle would have been avoided could they but have remembered, and seen the enduring significance of, that earliest stab of self-awareness and desire, to which some other was essentially, though vaguely, present. It may be that the accurate remembering of childhood is a gift reserved for our epoch. Wittgenstein observed that when Augustine in his *Confessions* thinks he is remembering how he first learned to speak, he is really describing how an adult, who already knows a language, learns a new one.

Our great philosophies start with 'the individual'. This sounds fine, except that 'the individual' means 'the self *and not the other*'. After all, says the philosopher, there must be some method, and the best place to start seems to be 'someone', an individual or a self. So let's think about him: his desires, fears and potential. We'll get to 'the other', to relationships, later.

Later is too late. 'The other' is already present to the self, as the meaning-giver for the self's most intimate and essential desire. If I am not making an oblique reference to others and their hoped-for acceptance, I am not really talking about the mind of that child, that adolescent, that young adult, that old man or woman. Once a philosophy of the self has been constructed without finding the true bridge to the other, a further mistake is made. People say: 'This self-centred thinking never gets to the other. Don't let's start with the self any more. Let's start with society.' Go ahead: you'll find you never reach the self! You're just making the reverse error. We have to start with the self, but the real self, whose need to be himself is the hunger for acceptance by others.

41

There is no problem of getting from the self to the other. The self has the other present to him as the condition of his self-esteem. The maturing of that original state of other-presence, from being a vague, oblique, self-supporting other, to being a definite, direct, self-inviting other, is the coming into love which is the climate of the mature self.

Hegel's Master-Slave parable fits beautifully into this schema. The Master is someone who has grown in self-awareness, and so in the need to be affirmed; while his perception of the other has remained at the vague, oblique, me-supporting stage of childhood. For Hegel, the Master's 'other' has that minimal otherness required for any self-esteem. That 'minimal otherness' is precisely the way the other is seen when we are 'minimal', tiny. The child enslaves others appropriately. The Master continues this enslavement inappropriately. What should be love has declined into power.

The task of maturing is the contrary transformation, of power into love, of the tyrannical infant into the loving adult. This transformation takes many forms. For instance, when a person has fallen in love and the other has not responded, the other has power over him, power which will only resolve into love if the beloved who is exerting it responds. The power-love scale is the scale of our ever-changing negotiation of our other-centred needfulness, and up and down it we go.

Sexual passion is a bridge between power and love. It raises people above themselves to be powerful to each other as the cause of desire. This power can change to tenderness, and vice versa. Therefore people sometimes take a bewildering plunge from extreme sexual tenderness to the infliction of savage cruelty and sometimes very devious manipulation. Sado-masochism is the contemporary sexual form of Hegel's Master-Slave parable.

14. A Further Look at the West

The following considerations develop the theme of the previous chapter:

1. Whether we like it or not, our western systems of thought have a profound shaping influence on our minds. Permeating the culture through many translations, social, political, aesthetic and religious, they give the guidelines whereby we articulate our experience. They mediate between the privacy of the self and the objective public world. However important some feeling may be to me, if it doesn't make it to the public world I shall lose grip of its importance. The having of feeling and the naming of feeling are intimately interlocked. The naming is largely in the control of the culture, which is fashioned by and in turn fashions the work of outstanding creative thinkers.

2. It is everybody's experience, however poorly recognized, that we desire above all to be desired by one we desire. In other words, the condition of being in love in one way or another is *the* sought-after condition.

3. None of our great philosophies is centred on love; so none of them reproduces this most basic fact.

4. Thus we have here a strident example of the non-permission by the culture for the articulation, as central to human life, of what everyone is after. The most sought-after consummation does not make it to the public world as the organizing centre of our culture.

5. This anomaly leaves people divided between the paramount private importance of the need to be in love and their public world which does not recognize this importance.

6. This betrayal of universal feeling by the culture has taken a further disastrous step through the decline of the controlling philosophy into materialism. This decline was inevitable, for the recognition of what we desire to be for each other is the primary and indispensable source for the recognition of spirit. A philosophy which does not make this recognition will, however spiritual its

43

language, decline into materialism. From Hegel the path to Marx is inevitable. The main purpose of this paragraph, however, is to accentuate the present divide in people between their private experience and the shaping culture.

7. The central concept of Christianity is love. The gospel is the proclamation that our need to be desired by one we desire is met by the God whom we above all desire since he is our very reason for existing. Our gospel-proclaimed desiredness in his eyes is the total fulfilment of that need to be in love which is the constitution of us as humans.

8. Alas, this message to man in his essential needfulness comes to one imprisoned in a cultural lie about himself, which consists in denying that needfulness. We have a Comedy of Errors which can be represented by a triangle whose points are: What the gospel is about: love/What everyone is after: love/What our culture says about us: not centred in love.

How are we to hear God's word of love to us, we who have banished love, our most universally sought-after grail, into a wistful private world? Before we start talking about the irrelevance of the gospel to modern man, let us consider the irrelevance to modern man of the culture in which he is imprisoned. To that culture, not to its hapless prisoner, the gospel is irrelevant, and appropriately so. Let us avoid the awful blunder of adjusting the gospel to make it relevant to that culture. This blunder is more easily made than we may think, for our western love-denying culture has its own version of the self it has thus privatized. To privatize is to *keep* private what starts private and desires to be public: in this case your and my and everybody's felt need to be desired by the one we desire. Whereas the truly private self desires to become public (in gospel language, to come into the Kingdom), the culturally privatized self has nothing but itself. To this isolated self the culture speaks of self-actualization. It is fatally easy for the minister of the gospel to make his message relevant to the culturally privatized self by making of it a traditionally hallowed form of self-actualization, an improving meditation technique with Jesus for its mantra. I have repeatedly fallen into this trap.

This amounts to making of Christianity the chaplain to what is now an inordinately selfish and world-devouring culture. By contrast, a true Christian spirituality will awaken us painfully to the impoverished victims of this culture, both ourselves and those in the world which we are impoverishing.

44

15. Self-Valuing and Confrontation

We have considered self-valuing in its full flowering, which is in love. To get an adequate idea of the centrality of self-valuing, we have also to see it in the context of confrontation. We introduce this chapter with the provocative question: Is God on the side of the poor?

My answer depends on my perception of the world. If I see 'the rich' and 'the poor' as two categories with no interaction between them, God is not on the side of either. On the other hand, if the rich are seen as exploiting the poor, I must say that infinite justice, integrity, goodness and truth are on the side of the exploited.

Is this my perception? Is the world that way? 'The world' is a vastly complicated reality, but certain principles can be disengaged. Insofar as the world is a network of interdependences controlled only by the profit-motive, the tendency is for the rich nations to become richer, the poor poorer. Insofar as the multinational corporations are controlled by the profit-principle, without external check, they are bound to go wherever labour is cheapest. Some very serious research tends to the conclusion that there is enough potential food in the world; what reduces whole areas to starvation is not natural scarcity but massive displacements of capital resources through the operation of the profit-motive without restraint.

In other words, much of the poverty in the world is a condition induced in some groups of people by others. Anyone who believes that God is justice and truth must see him as identifying in a special way with the victims. It is what any decent person feels when he sees someone being beaten up, and God is infinitely more 'decent' than we are. It should also go without saying that neither a decent person nor a loving God wishes in those circumstances to see the victim taking a merciless revenge. The Bible sees God this way. The prophets of Israel were always inveighing against the rich as the powerful who oppressed the powerless poor.

The fact that oppression of the powerless by the powerful goes back to the Bible reminds us that the phenomenon is world-wide and world-old. With very few exceptions, whatever civilization and order we have had in this world have been secured by the powerful, the prestigious, and always at the cost of some oppression. What we call a 'good' order arises when the powerful, secure in their position, can afford to humanize the system to some extent. In this corrupt world, the good is the mellow. Thus the English monarchy, once it had put the barons in their place, could create the *Pax Domini Regis,* the peace of the Lord King, in the land. Edward III called in Dominican scholars to help him frame laws based on mercy and justice.

We cannot understand much in the way of social justice unless we take stock of this formidable, world-wide and world-old phenomenon of oppression of the powerless by the powerful. No one who hasn't thought deeply about power can have much to say about social justice, unless he or she is a saint: saints can break most rules.

Hegel discovered the deep motivation behind this phenomenon. He saw that this motivation was not, at root, greed, the mere lust to possess, but the desire to feel more significant. Here is how Hegel builds up his idea. A person wants to feel significant. He wants to feel that his life is his own to enjoy, but he soon comes to realize that he cannot feel significant all by himself. He needs another, because the person is meaningless to himself in total isolation. This looks very like the need 'to be myself for another' which we have found central to human desire. Yet Hegel is not talking about love, but about a strategy used by something in us that does not want to share, at least not yet.

What is that strategy? Hegel's imaginary person employs another to supply that minimum of 'other-ness' necessary to enhance his own self-importance. The other person is there mainly for that purpose, to be the reassuring echo of the first person's sense of his own significance. In short the other is the slave, the retinue, the extension, of the first person. Hegel is thus launched on his famous Master-Slave image, which gave Marx the model for the class conflict. It is awe-inspiring to read the chapter in *The Phenomenology of Mind* where Hegel develops this idea. This highly sophisticated piece of philosophic reasoning is at the origin of a movement which has affected more human lives than any other in modern times. So much for the view that intellectuals have no impact on society and its history!

The Slave, in this deal, has no sense of his own life as significant. More accurately, his significance *is* to enhance the Master's significance. There is a certain payoff, for in order to prevent the Slave from developing any personal responsibility or sense of himself as a person, the Master looks after all his wants. The Slave hasn't a care in the world, and that's rather pleasant. This state of affairs does not last. The Slave begins to get a sense of his own significance. He begins, in his mind, to imitate the Master's confident style. Humanness is catching. The Slave wants 'to do it too'.

The Master observes this subtle change in the Slave with great disquiet. Obscurely he feels in it the ebbing of his own glory. His great strategy of self-importance is coming apart. The Master tries to resist this development. He tries to keep the Slave down. The more he does this, the more he finds himself preoccupied with the Slave as another centre of conscious significance appearing on the scene as a threat. The Master's consciousness begins to centre on the Slave and what he is doing, just as at first the Slave's consciousness was centred on the Master and his doings. The roles are beginning to be reversed. A certain slave-quality, a dependence-quality, is beginning to appear in the Master. Eventually, if the Master continues to try to maintain his dominance, the roles are reversed. The Master is enslaved by the necessity of enslaving the other; the Slave is the master of the situation; he has won the battle for significance.

Hegel is really talking about *power,* examining its very essence, seeing how it emerges and how it behaves. Power is a person's, or a people's, sense of significance seeking to advance itself with another, other than by the way of love. It is the sense of personal significance as it fares in a climate of inequality and struggle. It is personal significance not in gift to another but in confrontation.

Confrontation has many shades of meaning, or, if you prefer, it can take many forms. At the beginning of our story it takes the form of the Master imposing his sense of his significance on the Slave. The Master confronts the Slave with his importance, which he requires the Slave to recognize. As the Slave begins to get his act together, we have another form of confrontation: he is not yet imposing himself on the Master, but rather facing him, forcing the

Master to recognize him. If the process goes all the way, the Slave ends up imposing himself on the Master.

Between the first phase and the last there is an infinity of degrees in the confrontation. Furthermore, the story does not have to go all the way. It can reach a state of very subtle mutual tolerance, with all sorts of unspoken bargains. Finally there is the possibility that, in the stability afforded by this trade-off, a new mutual respect may grow. This is the beginning of love, the true, most desirable and most enhancing condition of the sense of significance between people. We have a transformation of power into love.

Power, then, is a very complicated and variegated phenomenon, but we can give a definition: Power is the sense of personal significance corroborated by the concern of another, by another's having to take me seriously. In contrast, love is the sense of personal worth experienced as enhanced by and enhancing another. So power and love are two modes of the working of the human drive to feel significant. We shall shortly be exploring the third great mode of this working, guilt.

Human life being complicated, power and love are both factors constantly to be taken into account. No marriage, for instance, can reach its full flowering without continual attention to both, with only a gradual growth from a power-situation into a love-situation. It is simplistic to think in terms of love alone. It is also simplistic to think that the Master-Slave story has to go all the way, as described by Hegel. This is the fallacy of Marx, who sees the process as inevitably climaxing in the reversal of roles, the 'dictatorship of the proletariat'.

We can now pinpoint the two commonest over-simplifications: simplification by the oppressor and simplification on behalf of the oppressed. The oppressor will tend to say, at least if he is a Christian: 'The class conflict is wrong. It is un-Christian. What we need is love, reconciliation.' He says this because he is afraid. He thinks that once the oppressed get any power, they'll do a pushover and reverse the roles. Strange paradox. Though he talks about love, he is assuming the truth of the essentially unloving doctrine that there is only the Master-Slave relationship or its reversal. He doesn't understand that the acquisition of some power by the oppressed can stop at forcing the oppressor to recognize their claims, can reach a healthy bargaining stage. This is the essence of the union theory, though it is abused by unions, just as capitalists abuse their power.

48

The simplification on behalf of the oppressed is to say that the only way is out-and-out revolution, the slam bid, the pushover, the reversal of the Master-Slave relationship. This simplification is based on exactly the same mistake as that of the oppressors: not to see that there is a stage of strong, irreversible confrontation which does not have to move on to all-out conflict, with one of the wrestlers throwing the other out of the ring.

The most fatal confusion, made by both right and left, is between confrontation and conflict. Conflict is to be avoided where possible; confrontation is to be sought where possible. This confusion is due to a very strong and widespread tendency to have a purely negative view of power. I asked a few students to define power, and all gave negative definitions, like 'manipulation of people', 'brainwashing', 'control of mass media'. But power is positive, and indispensable in human society, although nearly always to some extent abused. *'Abusus non tollit usum'* is a useful thing to remember: that something is abused does not invalidate its use. Acton's famous and usually misquoted saying, 'Power tends to corrupt, absolute power corrupts absolutely', is over-used, letting people off the hook of thinking about this dynamite called power. *Dynamis* is the Greek word for power. Power is the enormously variegated link between anarchy and love. It is the manifestness of people in their value to each other, short of the full flowering of that mutual manifestness in love.

16. A Time for Logic

Is the human self, now understood to be absolute, the only spiritual being? Am I, in my absoluteness, alone? If there are spiritual beings on other worlds, are they, with us, the only spiritual being?

If so, then I am God.
But, so far as I know, I did not make the world.
Therefore I am not God.
Therefore I am not alone.

This piece of logic has exploded on me like a bombshell and will explode on our culture. Here are the two ingredients for the explosion. On the one hand, no culture has become so convinced as ours that the self is absolute. We have a much more developed consciousness of what is offended against in the oppression and manipulation of peoples. I mean the absoluteness of the person, which forbids his being *used* for any purpose, which forbids us to regard the person as a means to an end. I do not depend for my me-ness on anybody or anything. In the current bewilderment over moral values, the person is emerging as the one moral absolute. The present Pope, incidentally, is a strong personalist. That makes him a good pope for this time.

Now for the second ingredient. Our culture, since the collapse of the *ancien régime* two centuries ago, has rigorously excluded the transcendent from serious public scientific consideration. It has privatized the religious sense. When, impelled by the personalism of our culture, I ask 'Am I, so exalted, the one absolute in a universe of relatives, alone?', the anti-transcendence belief of our culture answers: 'Yes, you are. God is an outgrown myth.' Thus the culture has me thinking of myself as absolute and on my own. The catalyst which triggers the logical explosion is: 'In that case I must be God.' Then the cat is out of the bag, for I am obviously not God.

50

Stay in the logic. Don't say: 'Therefore there is a God.' That blows the whole experience. Give the argument's conclusion: therefore we are not alone. Let it sink in. Slowly a new concept of the person emerges, as a metaphysical companionship. A total re-structuring of our knowledge is required once you accept this new definition of a person: a person is a relationship of which the other is infinite. What will the Psychology Department make of that?

There are moments in life, perhaps rare, when logic is necessary, when we need to be 'called' for trying to have our cake and eat it.

17. Forms of the Question

Some recapitulation and expansion of the perspective of Part I is now in order. This first part attempts to formulate a question which would put into words the deepest and most life-shaping desire of the human being. I can discern three possible formulations of this question.

1. Concentrating on the passionate conviction of our worth as humans which motivates the whole human enterprise, we ask how that conviction relates to our unknowingness of our origin, purpose and destiny. Far from this unknowingness only casting doubt upon the conviction of our significance, it *is* its heightening. My sense of myself becomes a sense of the significance of my experience through my certainty that this sense of self is in others too. The 'we' is in the 'I', and the 'I' in the 'we'. This is the birth of language, both in the child and in the race. This communicated sense of self is celebratory, and celebration implies a sense of mystery. If mystery, then, is the very quality of our self-esteem, it makes sense to say that this mystery in the human owes its fascination to the mystery of our very existence, that it yearns toward the ground of our being. The nearest analogue we have is the enormous expectation a person has of another who has become absorbingly attractive to him.

This form of the question can now be developed. The sense that I am absolute is not the sense of myself as an individual. Nor is it the sense of myself as a member or example of a species. It is the shared celebration of human life which lifts the sense of myself to the heights of mystery. Life does not become fascinating until that moment, epitomized for philogeny and ontogeny by the birth of language, when it is realized that the dream of myself is the dream in other minds. It is only as 'in the others too' that the experience of being a self has that quality which compels us to say that it is absolute, unique, non-derivative. 'Interesting' means 'shared'. At

52

the moment of the birth of language the image suddenly attended to more closely is, indivisibly, 'the image intended by the common sounds and gestures and therefore in the other minds as well'.

As long as it remains unnamed, the conscious flow of life does not have this quality of fascination which it acquires in the very moment that it yields its privacy to the world of language. The astounding claim for a creature's self-awareness, that it is a reality which holds its own in the world, is only made or meaningful with the break into the daylight of language. Yet it is precisely as 'holding its own in the world' that our self claims absoluteness. If I stake out such a claim, the claim is to absoluteness. To dare to say that anything so other than nature and so feeble in comparison as 'I' can make a counter-claim is to make an all-the-way claim. It is through the presence of us to each other enacted in language that I have that solidity, that sense of objectivity, which grounds the counter-claim that 'I' am an order, a world, over against the world of nature.

When we say that the self knows itself as absolute, we are referring to the whole human enterprise of communication and celebration, which is wonderful and tells him that he is wonderful. It is as a participant that he knows himself as an irreducible, absolute value. Apart from that participation there is certainly consciousness, but not that significant consciousness which calls for our recognition as absolute.

2. A term such as 'the unknown' is vague; but there is a sense of that term which describes how the cause of our being, which is the cause of being, is felt by us. To what we probably have to call the soul, 'the unknown' means the origin. It means my unknown, our unknown. 'The unknown' is the soul's code-name for that which constitutes it in being. This code has become strange to us, as have our myths, those stories we told about ourselves before we learned to lie. So the life-laden question becomes: 'Is the unknown the knowing one?' An affirmative answer would totally transform a person's life.

3. Our sense of the absoluteness of the person, which grows out of the communication and celebration matrix, can be contrasted with everything other than persons. This contrast impels me to ask: 'Am I, are we, in this absoluteness, alone? Am I (and any galactic self-aware beings there might be) the only spiritual, absolute reality?' If so, then I am God. Clearly I am not God. Therefore I am

53

not alone. I am involved in a companionship which liberates me from the burden of being God by being with God.

The experience of myself as absolute is community-based. The opening of the self to a God beyond the self depends on the existence of this community base. Thus the ultimate relationship, the relationship that the person is, at once differs from all our known relationships and gathers them all into their primary significance, which is the elevation of the self to absolute status. This is why God, in coming through to a person, is calling a people into being. The intensely personal nature of God's revelation to key figures in the Old Testament, far from being opposed to the dominant emphasis on the people as a people, is the very strength in that emphasis. It is only people who have forgotten all about themselves who find a paradox here.

Each of these three approaches has its merits. It is only by means of a complementarity of suggestiveness that this deepest movement of the soul may be persuaded to find words, to become a question. The first approach deduces the 'erotic' relationship with the unknown God, while the second and third approaches evoke it.

PART II—THE SHADOW

18. The Shadow Between People

The second part of this book is about guilt. In my theology class we assembled a blackboard description of guilt, composed of such words as 'helpless', 'ashamed', 'deprived', 'degraded', 'low', 'lonely'. All these words, descriptive of intense moments or moods of the self, imply the presence of the other, some strongly, some lightly. Somehow, another is being 'failed'. This suggests that we may get our root meaning for guilt by recalling the positive relationship to the other set up by our basic desire 'to be significant to'. We can then define guilt as the negating of this relationship, the 'counter-pull' to the positive 'pull' to be myself for another.

What is the relationship between the positive desire 'to be myself for another' and the opposing pull? When I surrender to the opposing pull, am I simply reversing the direction of the positive? Am I simply choosing not to be myself for the other? Am I simply opting out from my desire to be myself for the other?

No. I cannot simply opt out from this desire. This desire *is* me. It is the thrust of my identity. To opt out of it would be to switch off my desire to be significant; this I cannot do, for I cannot cease to want to be myself. When I give way to the negative impulse, the positive pull continues and I am out of harmony with it. I now experience the pull as making me unhappy. The claim of the other upon me is no longer inviting me to be myself for him or her, but accusing me of failing to be so. Guilt is the sense of failing another or others. Guilt is the failure of love.

Most people would agree with this description. To understand it I have to remember that 'being myself for the other' is the direction of my central life thrust; the sense of failing in this is a sense of failing in myself and as myself, of failing myself. If I forget this, I shall say another person is making me feel guilty, so that I must get away from this ugly situation. That is what most psychological systems say, because they are not based on the central and unalterable orientation of the self towards the other in love. Because of this orientation, guilt is not just something induced in me by another, but a state of affective impotence in myself. In guilt, I am 'not functioning properly' as a person-for-persons. This is the radical guilt: unhappy unlove.

This situation is complicated by the fact that often people make me feel guilty by making an improper demand, and that this *is* a situation I should try to get away from. What is happening in this case? The other person is trying to be to me what other persons are for the child, a needed support for the undeveloped self. What we call peer pressure is the attempt of our peers to keep us, and them, infantile. It is a serious mistake to take this kind of guilt as the norm, as what guilt fundamentally is. We have already seen the error of arguing that, since being infantile means being dependent on others, being adult means being independent of others. Our true development is not from dependence to independence but from dependence to true relationship, from the dependence of children of the interdependence of adults, from the extended womb to the community of persons. The concept of guilt as essentially infantile is precisely the mistake of calling our development a growth from dependence to independence, to a state without guilt.

In other words, there is infantile guilt and adult guilt, just as there is the infantile form of the positive desire for significance and the adult form. Infantile guilt is the shadow of the joyous infant eros, of the child 'grasping at kisses and toys' (Eliot): the sudden stab of loneliness, of being left out, abandoned, of a power-cut in the generous adult current of love. It is the passive sense of being unloved. Adult guilt is the shadow of adult love. It is the active sense of being unloving.

Guilt is our most important negative feeling. Not surprisingly, it turns out to be the perversion of the most important of our positive feelings: the desire to be myself for another or others.

Thus we can organize this book so far round three definitions, all centred on the basic thrust of self-esteem:

Love is the self-esteem fulfilled in mutual enhancement of life.
Power is self-esteem coming into successful confrontation.
Guilt is self-esteem failing in its growth into love.

Note

The 'Gestalt Prayer' was composed by Fritz Perls as a poetic summing-up of Gestalt Therapy. I've seen it on at least one banner:

I do my thing, and you do your thing.
I am not in this world to live up to your expectations
And you are not in this world to live up to mine.
You are you and I am I,
And if by chance we find each other, it's beautiful.
If not, it can't be helped.[1]

This prayer illustrates the contemporary confusion over guilt. It is a beautiful half-truth, for it assumes that the only 'expectations' people can have of each other are those improper expectations which keep us in infantile guilt. Correspondingly, it assumes that the only guilt people feel is the infantile guilt of not living up to others' expectations. Predictably, love shows up in this picture as a happy accident having no place in the structure of being a person. By way of contrast, St Paul describes mutual adult expectations succinctly: 'Owe no man anything, but to love one another' (Rom. 13:8).

[1] Frederick S. Perls, *Gestalt Therapy Verbatim* (Moab, UT: Real People Press, 1969), p. 40.

19. Chasing the Shadow

Guilt is a slippery fish. Here are some hooks.

1. Guilt is the sense of failing another. It is the most personal sense of failure I experience, because my very feeling of personal worth is 'in another's eyes'. As my sense of worth is of 'worth to', so my sense of unworthiness is of 'unworth to'.

2. If love is feeling good in the presence of another, guilt is feeling bad in the presence of another.

3. Guilt is love in reverse vainly trying to reverse itself.

4. Guilt is love gone sour.

5. Guilt is an emotional impotence.

6. Guilt is when all that is left of another's calling on me is the 'ought', the 'should'. 'Should' plus 'can't' equals guilt.

7. As long as we're stuck with guilt, we try to pay, and we can never pay enough. Guilt is the currency of love, gone into inflation.

8. Doubt of our worth to another is guilt. I may not think I think all that poorly of myself, when I just sit down alone; but when I think of myself in my relations with others, I can see my bad self-concept in operation.

20. Casting the Shadow

One very important aspect of the feeling of guilt is that the other, the person I am failing, appears strangely unattractive. I say 'strangely', because this unattractiveness does not reside in the person as part of his character in my eyes, remaining the same whatever happens. It is more like an appearance which the person suddenly takes on as a result of a change of feeling in me. This change is not coming to dislike the person, but the quite different, guilty feeling of failing the person. Dislike is masking my real feeling, which is guilt. A very nasty character in Dostoevsky's *The Brothers Karamazov* says of someone: 'I did him a bad turn years ago and I've had a grudge against him ever since.' That hits it exactly. We tend to think and speak ill of people whom we are failing.

I wonder why this happens? Perhaps the feeling of guilt is so unpleasant that, rather than face it in itself, we invent a justifying external cause: 'After all he is a sonofabitch.' Guilt transposed into dislike is easier to live with than guilt in the pure state. But of course it's worse for me. I've compounded my guilt with a lie: the lie that 'I just don't happen to like the guy.'

This phenomenon appears in politics. We form a group to oppose an administration for its policy on some issue. We assume that no one in the administration would be willing to talk frankly with us; we make no real attempt to approach them. This automatic and unconsidered moral outlawing of the administration produces a sense of guilt, of a failure in communication to which we have willingly assented. This sense of guilt suddenly suffuses the administration, in our eyes, with a certain inhuman quality. They become caricatures of humans, inviting the debased art of the poster designer. It can go on like this for years, even for generations, so that children are born into this picture-book stereotype of the enemies of our class or creed.

Racial and sexual prejudice is also describable in these terms.

The real evil happens unnoticed. It is the first reaction of guilt at separating myself from the other. Then this first movement supports and disguises itself by making the other race or sex look alien and threatening. The disaffection (dis-affection, strangling of affection) of guilt throws the other out of human focus into caricature. All war propaganda operates this mechanism.

Simone Weil points out something we do not like to recognize: we recoil from someone who has fallen into great misfortune. The reason surely is that when disaster happens to someone, I feel guilty at not being with him, at separating myself from him. That's the first, unnoticed movement. Then this move supports and disguises itself by making the person look ugly. Guilt has thrown the person out of human focus into the other world of the outcast.

A similar mechanism produces the feeling known as *ressentiment,* the French word for resentment, used by Max Scheler and since found to be an important concept for social analysis.[2] An initial failure to enjoy something gets recorded in the subconscious and comes out in a certain bitter feeling at the sight of people enjoying that thing. The fox in the fable who could not reach the grapes went away saying, 'They were sour anyway!' The same process: first the failure to connect, then this painful sense of failure makes itself bearable under the disguise of dislike of that pleasure in other people. A great deal of moral condemnation of the pleasures of the rich stems from this source.

The first step towards the dissolving of guilt is to step back from this last stage, to realize that this is not just a case of 'not happening to like the fellow'. The second step is to realize that the ugliness the other person or group has in our eyes is of a very special kind, being induced in them by our sense of failing them. We have to get used to that very unpleasant feeling we often have, of failing another and thus making him appear ugly. Especially in a narcissistic culture like ours, people tend to feel surrounded with other people as emblems of their own failure to come out of themselves.

It is painful to catch ourselves doing this, but there is a positive side. It is much more difficult to grow to like someone I simply dislike than to come to like someone whom I have been making unlikeable. In the former case we have a given unlikeableness; in the lat-

[2] *Ressentiment,* ed. Lewis Coser, tr. William W. Holdheim (New York: Schocken, 1972).

ter an induced unlikeableness; and I am the inducer. A deliberate show of affection in the latter case might totally change the situation between us, because all that is standing in the way is the domino of my own placing. In the case of someone I've always disliked and never got along with, there's a great deal more in the way.

What are the ingredients of this guilt-induced unlikeableness? First, it has to do with perception: the person suddenly looks unpleasant, and the suddenness accentuates the perceptual quality. Second, this perception is produced by the damming-up of a natural flow of affection, by an affective jam. My failure, my affective impotence, has thrown the other person out of focus for me, so that what I have before me is not a human being but a caricature. In this caricature I rest as an excuse for my original failure in affectivity. We often find ourselves with images of people thrown out of focus for us by our failure to meet them. They are affectively thrown out of focus. Until we change, we cannot see them any more in the way that humans need and desire to see other humans.

It would be intriguing to see if we could trace this process at work in our attitude to a mystery very obscurely perceived to be the reason, meaning and purpose of our being. Could we do so, we would be performing a great service to ourselves and all Christians. We would be learning to recognize, in ourselves, in human society today, that religious guilt whose dissolving by God's love is the central theme of the gospel; to recognize religious guilt as a human unhappiness, not as something from which the Church tells us we suffer.

21. The Shadow on God

In guilt the other is experienced not as presence but as pressure. Under this pressure I feel a powerlessness to love. The felt powerlessness to love is the very nerve of guilt. Because my root inclination is to enter into relationships, I tend to interpret the unlovableness of someone as something I am producing by strangling this inclination. This makes me feel guilty. Although there is only a limited sense in which it is true to say that the unlovableness of another is my fault, it is something I can never be happy about. This unhappiness is a feeling of guilt.

When something is going badly wrong with an intimate relationship, we experience this 'ugliness of the other' in an intense way. Suddenly the beloved can appear hateful. This is due to the sudden failure of my normal love-current, which leaves the beloved before me in all his or her closeness and involvement in my life, while I am powerless to respond. Guilt is acute when the intimate other becomes alien. In all guilt, the other appears alien. Guilt is when the other changes from partner to alien. Because partnership is natural and congenial to me, is the way my life wants to flow, this 'alienation' of the partner is experienced by me as a contradiction with myself. This self-contradiction, this inner friction of the spirit, is the experience of guilt.

Is there an 'other' in our life who is *the* other to which our whole being looks for meaning, and whose becoming unlovable to us would thus constitute the most radical and universal form of guilt? Recall the universal human phenomenon of how each person sees himself as special and prizes himself and his life above all things. Our sense of ourselves as precious is a question addressed to whatever it is that is the reason why we are: do I have reason for being; am I significant in the ultimate design of the universe? The 'target' of this question is the other about whom I asked, the other on whose 'smile' depends all my meaning.

How does this other 'appear ugly' to me? It does so to the extent that I receive from it no assurance; to the extent that my life in this world seems merely the plaything of blind forces; to the extent that I am not comfortable with my life the way it is given me beyond my control, with my body, or my sex, or my sexuality, or any of the other innumerable things which go to form the given me, the me I can't do a thing about. In other words, all the ordinary human feelings of doubt and dissatisfaction and disaffection with one's lot bring about that 'ugliness of the other' which we experience in all guilt. In this case it is the original other, so its ugliness reflects the original guilt.

This guilt is the crippling in us of that in-love-ness with the all-powerful mystery which belongs to our very constitution as self-aware, self-fascinated, questing, questioning beings. It is an original cosmic love-affair gone sour. It is the all-embracing mystery experienced not as presence but as pressure. It is the sense of 'unworth to' that mystery. It is an emotional impotence where our deepest life is concerned. It is when the call of the mystery is associated with law, not love.

The history of religion affords ample documentation of this 'appearing ugly and alien' to man of the original other: as the God, or gods, who demanded every sort of payment and self-infliction on the part of man. Nowhere is the definition of guilt as 'the inflationary currency of love' so powerfully verified as in the history of religion.

22. An Anatomy of Guilt

Although our sense of worth, which motivates all our behaviour, finds its proper development only in relationships, where it reveals itself as the enhancing of life for self and others, there is inherent in self-awareness a possibility of experiencing myself as isolated, without any connection with life or with others. This possibility is frequently actualized. The self which normally and properly goes out to engage with other selves recedes to a point of pure self-awareness and exists in relation to itself alone. The sense of self which in healthy states is an essential ingredient in an other-embracing experience becomes all that there is. There is a kind of loss of nerve, of the nerve of life.

This withdrawal is the cause of guilt, for it brings a sense of failing the 'life' from which I am withdrawn. This may be a sense of robbery, of stealing my private life from the whole in which I am a participant. It may be a sense of the inferiority, the unworthiness, of this privatized life in respect of the life of the whole, of the life which is truly *of* the whole. An absolutely private life is a contradiction in terms. These two senses, of theft and of unworthiness, are closely connected and seem to merge into each other. The main point is that guilt is how I feel about some situation or person, some life-sharing encounter, from which I have withdrawn into my isolated selfhood.

I have often thought that the root of guilt is self-dislike; but this in its turn only arises through isolation. I don't look at all good to myself when I withdraw myself from any possibility of feeling good: that is, from all relationship. We are nearer the root of the matter when we derive guilt from self-isolation. It is the possibility, inherent in self-awareness, of withdrawal into pure, self-referred self-awareness which, when actualized, produces the primordial guilty relationship of a person to an other or others or to life as a whole.

Consider this shrinking back to pure self as occurring in the context of my total situation as a human being involved with mystery. If our sense of human life as of ultimate value is our sense of investment in an ultimate mystery (which is sensed as knowing and willing by a person awakening to the Spirit), what will that isolation be which consists in experiencing myself divorced from that life-giving context? It will be a state of total emptiness: self-awareness deprived not only of the enrichment of friends but of that more radical enrichment which is the very condition for a meaningful human existence. It will be a far deeper isolation than man can know in the human community. It is to be without any reason for being except what one can generate in isolation from within.

This is how I seek to understand, appropriate and mediate into today's culture the doctrine of original sin. The experience of original sin is produced by the withdrawing of the self from its primordial leanings towards ultimate mystery into an absolutely isolated self hood. So far I have equated the guilt of original sin with original sin itself, making of that guilt a radical condition which one could not go behind to a sin causing the guilt. I would now say that just as inter-human guilt is at least logically preceded by the 'sin' of withdrawing into isolated self-awareness, so the deeper guilt in respect of our very being is at least logically preceded by the sin of withdrawing into isolated self-awareness in respect of the mystery on which we in fact draw for all our sense of meaning and value.

The socio-cultural character of original sin is thus evident. If original sin means treating as non-existent the dependence of our sense of man's meaning and value on the ultimate mystery, it is in society as a whole, where the human sense of man's meaning and value is stored, expressed in institutions and in the whole cultural achievement, that we shall expect to find this non-acknowledgement, this conspiratorial silence as to the ultimate source of man's sense of his meaning and value. Original sin is the universal and socialized withdrawal of man from the mystery on which he yet continues to draw for all his meaning and value. Original sin is the socialized truncation of human life, the systematic reduction of the child of mystery to the banal world of man's own making.

Just as the sense of the person's absolute value arises through communication with other selves, so the sinful sense of being worthless is communicated. Just as every person has in himself the two movements, every culture carries on its communication network the two conflicting messages. The same culture which builds persons erodes them.

Here is another important connection. The person is *either* to be regarded as convinced of his worth and demanding recognition of it, *or* to be regarded as feeling worthless and asking to be made to feel worthful by others. Part I stressed the first option as the main thrust of personhood, but we can now locate the second. People often feel worthless and try, either by themselves or through others, to fill the void. This is the sin-element in us. Those books of popular psychology in which the bottom line is the need to be built up by others, the need to be 'stroked', are describing as normal what is really the sinful condition. Likewise the ideology of consumerism, whose bottom line is: 'You are worthless in yourself; you need our product.' More broadly still, we have to ask what basic presupposition about the nature of the person underlies our culture. Our culture exalts the freedom of the individual over the sense of obligation, and in so doing exalts the ability to do anything over the desire to do good. This makes 'the empty person' the culture's model. 'The empty person' is the work of sin.

Let me pursue this thinking further, in the interests of precision and depth, at the risk of a degree of repetition. Our sense of self-worth is blighted by a sense of unworth. Just as the sense of self-worth heads us towards God, the sense of unworth heads us away from God and is sin in its most radical meaning. If Hitler's Holocaust and Stalin's Gulag Archipelago have not taught us that the main aim of the power of evil is to persuade people that they are worthless, nothing will. The main meaning of sin has written itself out, for our generation, in fifty million tortured lives.

It is easy to misunderstand religious language about man's 'worthlessness before God'. What in God's eyes is worthless about me is the worth I substitute for what *I* see as worthless and God sees as beautiful because he makes it. A similar sense of worthlessness often accompanies falling in love, when I appropriately sense as worthless all the baggage of earned self-esteem acquired before love taught me my true worth. St Paul describes all his erstwhile legal righteousness as 'dung' now that he knows Jesus. Yet more often than not religious language, especially of the fundamentalist sort, wrongly tells us that we really are worthless in God's eyes. It is the task of theology here to make it quite clear that God is not a jerk and does not make junk. Religion has done much harm by endorsing people's wretched ideas of themselves, whereas it is precisely religion's job to cure people of this sin of self-negation.

Self-disesteem, then, is the root human evil. It has many shades: self-dislike, self-loathing, self-hate, self-destructiveness, death-wish, self-indifference and many more. The root is self-disesteem, the failure in that self-valuing which is and remains the very life of the sense of self. You cannot experience yourself at all without some sense of being valuable.

Traditional religious language, as well as common sense, sees guilt as the outcome of sin, as what it feels like to be in sin. I accept this immemorial perception of sin as the central thing wrong, with guilt seen as how our experience carries this central wrong and tries to deal with it. But the sin with which my analysis is concerned is that unaccountable inner negativity of which Paul writes in Romans 7:13ff. The guilt I find in human relations is a vague unhappiness generated by this root evil. Introduce into my picture the Baltimore Catechism's concept of sin, and you snarl it up badly: 'If you feel guilty in a situation, you must have committed a sin'! Guilt as I understand it is a failing of others and of God which has its deep root in self-negation. The guilt resulting from the doing of a specific wrong is only a focussing of a much deeper and wider sense of guilt whose source is our inner self-negation. Feeling worthless (sin) leads to feeling inadequate (guilt): 'acting worthless' leads to feeling downright inadequate.

Since guilt is essentially a jarred or embittered relationship it is only dissolved by a recovery of true relationship. In a recovered relationship the feeling of poor self-worth in one or both of the parties is prevailed over by the true sense of self. Only thus is guilt dissolved. People try to get rid of guilt in all sorts of ways, but it doesn't work. They try to shift the burden of guilt from self onto other; or they try to 'pay', which incidentally is one way of making the other feel guilty. Only the recovery of love dissolves guilt.

As to the ultimate relationship: if the sense of self-worth, fully operative in a community-based appreciation of the value of the self, leads to the realization that I am not alone, to what will a sense of personal unworth lead? To the conclusion that I am ultimately alone. The voice of sin in us says: 'Yes, you are alone. In all this universe you are ultimately alone. You will crawl into a hole and die, alone. You are no more than an animal after all'.

Just as a person's sense of worthlessness 'jars' his relationship with another, his sense of worthlessness jars his relationship with the huge, positive, loneliness-denying mystery we call God. This relationship never disappears, any more than the sense of worth ever disappears. It remains, but cankered, jarred, embittered. The relationship with God is infected with sin (unworth) and takes on a guilty quality which spoils its free love-quality.

Further, just as in human relationships, guilt in face of the ultimate tries to cure itself by making God look ugly or angry or somehow fearsome. Thus God is not only the loving one who affirms life, but the ogre who has to be placated with sacrifices. The story of Abraham and Isaac shows wonderfully how Abraham, the father of Jewish, Christian and Islamic faith, experienced the breakthrough from the guilt-side of God (who, Abraham thought, demanded the sacrifice of his only son) to the love-side of God. Yet the Abrahamic step was only a beginning. All religion manifests the dual quality in God corresponding to the dual self-estimate of man, with one exception: the new experience of God which Jesus had and gave to his followers after his death and in his resurrection.

23. On Sin

If guilt is the resultant in respect of the 'other' of my yielding to the tendency of self-aware being to 'think isolated', and if this yielding is what is meant by sin, we must ask a further question. How are we to categorize the *attitude* of sin, of withdrawing into isolation? Is it 'malicious', or 'wicked', or 'malevolent', or 'rebellious', or 'perverse', or 'hostile'? The list could be extended. All these condemnatory descriptions make some reference, if only obliquely, to 'the other', to that objective reality which the sinner flouts, or ignores, or disregards, or seeks to destroy, or seeks to steal. Thus none of them succeeds in focussing on that sheer withdrawal into isolation which is the essence of sin.

This fact should warn us of how difficult it is to touch the essence of sin. It is much easier to think of sin as an attack on something positive, and this we regularly do in all our denunciations of moral evil. Yet even the attack on the good, even the attempt to get it out of the way, is an engagement with the real, objective world; whereas sin, in its essence, is precisely a disengagement. Although we all know this disengagement well in ourselves and in each other, it is very hard to describe in terms of an attitude.

Indeed, it seems that this cannot be done. All attitudes envisage objects, whether of aversion or evasion or desire or hope or fear or whatever. This 'attitude', this stance, has no object. It is simply the closing-up of the self. On the other hand it would be a disastrous mistake to conclude that sin is not deserving of condemnation. On the contrary, the essence of sin escapes all the condemnatory descriptions because it is far worse than anything they convey. There are no words for the desire, which cannot really be called a desire, to be absolutely myself-for-myself-alone, absolutely isolated.

As the religious insight of the Old Testament matures into that of the New under the sublime influence of Jesus, the condition of the sinner is seen as calling for pity and compassion rather than for condemnation: not because the evil of sin is less emphasized but for the opposite reason that the evil of sin is far more apparent. In the New Testament it is at last understood that man can turn in on himself, find nothing and yet remain fixated. Rightly is this fact called a mystery of iniquity, with emphasis on the word mystery. People who grasp sin in these ultimate and tragic terms generally find themselves disposed to believe that there are Powers of Darkness beyond man. I merely remark this. It is not a necessary logical connection, but it seems that there is a connection. Incidentally, the scriptural context of the phrase 'mystery of iniquity' is the context of the diabolic (2 Thess. 2:7).

Thomas Aquinas says about evil generally and sin in particular that evil is not anything. It is an absence of what should be there, a *privatio boni*. For a stone to be without sight is not an evil, but for a man to be so is a physical evil. When it comes to the moral evil we call sin, Aquinas says that in itself it is motiveless and unintelligible. In terms of what I stand to gain by a sinful choice—wealth, power, pleasure—the motivation is abundant. But no one and nothing can account for that inner decision to be for myself alone, which silently underlies the swift spectacular action of the thief or of him who seeks power over men's souls. As a disciple of Lonergan once put it, 'The appropriate insight on the subject of sin is that no insight is here to be had.'

People have great difficulty with this thesis. Jung quarrelled with it all his life but, though he talked a great deal about evil, never understood it. He thought he could understand it as 'the shadow', the dark side of our life from which we flee; but that is not what evil is.

For some time I wondered whether guilt or fear is the more basic human evil. It has to be guilt, in so far as guilt is the symptom of sin which, unlike fear, is beyond our understanding. To forgive sin, truly to dissolve its guilt, is to enable the sinner to come out of his or her willed isolation into love. Even in the case of an injury done to another human being, enablement by the other is needed, just as the other's avowal of love is needed for a lover to take the 'second quantum leap'. It is the other, become lovable again, who dissolves guilt and forgives the injury. In the case of our primordial relationship with the source of all our belief in ourselves and our life, what a prodigious becoming-lovable-again that must be which leads man out of an immemorial captivity in sin into the love through which alone there is a world at all. This is the subject of Part III of this book.

Finally and crucially, while sin is the root of guilt, man is much more conscious of guilt in regard to God, or in regard to 'the universe' or 'the whole', than he is of sin. It is ever the symptom that appears, which is what symptom means.

PART III—JESUS

24. The Structure of the Guiltless Person Corresponds to the Gospel Story of Jesus

No one receives all of his life gratefully and joyfully from the source of being. A thousand experiences, and the memory of a race, lead a person to doubt the loving intentions of that source. All images of God are to some extent images of guilt. Our study of guilt helps to appreciate the momentous nature of Christianity, which believes in a state of humankind free of this universal blight. It sees that state as represented by a man who lived nearly two thousand years ago, Jesus of Nazareth. It sees all humankind as intended by its maker to come into that state.

From the beginning, Christians have believed that Jesus was 'without sin'. While there was much debate as to his precise nature theologically, this deep root of unique goodness was never in dispute. What does it mean to describe Jesus as 'without sin'? That will depend on what you mean by sin. If sin is simply the breaking of a law, then Jesus is the man who kept all the rules. I once heard a sermon in which the preacher pointed out that life at Nazareth must have been somewhat complicated by the fact that, while Joseph could say 'shit!' when he dropped a hammer on his toe, Jesus couldn't! That's not what sin is, as we have seen.

From my point of view the most important thing the New Testament says about Jesus is that he was 'without sin', 'like us in all things save sin' (Hebrews). Once we recognize sin as the universal negation-tendency in our lives, and not just as a breaking of divine rules, we can recognize in Jesus our true self totally liberated from 'the cancer that eats away the self'. At least we are able to see what would be the consequences of this freedom and in this sense to construct a psychology of Jesus. Here are three such consequences of freedom from sin and its resultant guilt.

First, this freedom is present at the deepest level, where a person confronts ultimate mystery. There would be a total, unimpeded intimacy with God. There would be no guilt in the relationship, no holding back and rendering the other fearsome and threatening. The self would flourish in its ultimate companionship with the infinite, in a total, grateful and joyful acceptance of one's being from the mystery, on which in consequence one casts no 'shadow'. There is a consciousness of the self as beloved of the mystery and of the mystery as unshadowed love and beauty. The sense of 'I am not alone' would be overpowering. There would be an almost inconceivable flourishing of the human person. The 'will of God' would not be for him a stern imposition, a fate, but his fulfilment—even to a horrible death.

Second, this liberated self would be open, in an inconceivably fuller way, to other selves as persons. Free of self-unworth at its very roots, he would contract no guilty or snarled-up relationships. Nobody would feel rejected, or pigeon-holed, or stereotyped: for these are all forms of guilt-projection, expressing our basic uneasiness with each other.

Third, this liberated self would be so convinced by his God-experience that this was the way life was meant to be, that he would come to see in his life no other meaning than the inauguration of this new, sin-free, guilt-free fellowship of men and women on this earth. Such a person would have the most intense sense that God, in his life, was doing something new, inaugurating a new age for humankind.

It is awe-inspiring to observe that these three salient characteristics of the sin-free person are precisely what the gospel story highlights in the life of Jesus. They can be summarized as God-intimacy, human intimacy and eschatology. First, Jesus is *par excellence* the intimate of God. He is said in the story of his baptism to have heard: 'You are my beloved son, in whom I am well pleased.' What was most remembered about the way he prayed was that he addressed the mystery as 'Abba', the affectionate diminutive form of 'Father'. The entitling of God as Father is by no means unique in and beyond Judaism, but the way Jesus does it, the 'tone of voice', the style, is unique. A Jewish boy's understanding of the word 'Abba' would be both more intimate and more respectful than we mean by 'Dad'. Furthermore, the very earliest records remember him as giving his life to fulfil the mysterious purpose of the 'will of God'.

The implication of this first consequence of Jesus' sinlessness is important. Jesus' consciousness of himself as 'beloved son' and of the mystery as 'Father' is something we can to some extent understand as representing all that man is, all that we are, in the mind of God. I say 'to some extent' because we can never fully understand this deepest reality of our life. We understand enough to say that our life is an enigma, written across every page of history as it twists this way and that, which becomes lucid in Jesus of Nazareth, beloved of God and knowing God as Parent.

Second, in the matter of human intimacy, the gospels lay special emphasis on Jesus' friendship with disreputable people: the hated tax-collectors, the despised (and used) prostitutes. Also strongly stressed is his friendship with women, a thing unheard-of in a religious teacher in that patriarchally religious society. 'This man eats and drinks with sinners' was the common taunt of decent religious people. This is sin-free behaviour. Sin, our fundamental uneasiness with ourselves, *needs* outcasts, rejected classes of persons, to 'make ugly' rather than face inwards to what Paul faced when he said: 'I am an enigma to myself.'

Third, on the question of eschatology, New Testament scholarship was revolutionzed early this century by the realization that the mind of Jesus, and of the gospel, was through-and-through 'eschatalogical', i.e., convinced that the new and eternal age of the Reign of God was at hand. Scholars increasingly realize that Jesus saw himself and his life as bringing in this new age of intimacy between God and humankind. The gospel story centres all Jesus' teaching, from the parables to the Sermon on the Mount, on the belief that the 'Reign of God' was now beginning on this earth with him. That Jesus' whole life and teaching centred on this conviction seems to be the one thing on which all New Testament scholars are agreed. This perspective poses the problem: Anyone who thinks of himself that way is either hugely deluded, psychotic or—something else. We understand what that 'something else' is when we realize that the vision of God on the part of a sin-free person would have to generate this conviction of a crucial mission. Thus the third main feature of the sinless person checks out with the gospel narrative.

In sum: an adequate anthropology, a picture of man as dynamized by the other-dialoguing eros and shadowed by guilt, enables us to get some understanding from within of the three salient features of the life of Jesus the *anthropos*. We are able to arrive at a psychological portrait of Jesus which is faithful to the New Testament's portrayal of that unique man.

25. The Turning Point of Religious History

What would be the effect of this new sort of man on his followers? His experience of God was catching. More specifically, they caught from him that sense of the beauty and goodness of nature, of the world, of life, of people, which is part of an open and guilt-free relationship with the mystery. Instead of a God who was remote and enigmatic, invoked in a formal way, there was a loving presence in everything; it brought people together; it promoted human flourishing everywhere.

All this was totally new. They felt that this total newness would soon come upon the whole world. His special way of talking about the Reign of God as starting here and now with his mission confirmed this. In short, they were on an ecstatic journey into world change, into apocalypse. Ocasional dark hints from him about a violent and bloody end were hastily brushed aside.

There is one implication which will prove to have definitive importance when, at the end of the story, we look back and discern the overall pattern. The 'God' they were now experiencing in the company of Jesus was incomparably more real than the God of traditional religion. It was as though they saw through the hallowed symbols and rituals to the burning reality itself. The corollary was: if this fails, if Jesus fails, if this movement piles up against the stone wall of this world, then God is finished. The only God now believable would have proved powerless. There would be no going back to the traditional God.

The movement came to nothing. Jesus was arrested and led away. In shame and confusion, utterly unprepared for so rude a turn of events, they fled. Those dark days would be a much more radical desolation than what we call the Dark Night of the Soul. The person who enters the Dark Night does not look back on such a heaven-on-earth as did the followers of Jesus. For them, God had involved himself so much in the life and the movement of Jesus that the failure of the movement was much more like the death of God than his mere absence.

With the death of God, something deep in the soul and very difficult to recognize or acknowledge also comes to an end. It is what is aroused in the soul of man by the thought of God's huge power compared with our weakness. It is an envy of God. It is Hegel's Master-Slave relationship in its most essential form. Envy, resentment, guilt: all these are woven into human religion and have been since the beginning. The metaphysical inequality between the creature and the Creator translates emotionally into the Master-Slave inequality. With God dead, with God *powerless,* with God no longer God, this movement of the soul would also cease.

This created a totally new possibility in these people: the possibility of hearing a new message from the mystery. The one obstacle to hearing the words, 'I simply love you and want you with me forever', has been removed; so the words could now be heard, if there were a God to speak them!

According to them, not only were they able to receive this new message, but they actually did receive it. How did they experience the filling of the vacuum left by the failure of Jesus and of God's Reign on earth? Their answer to this question is clear. They were revived from their total spiritual collapse by Jesus himself coming to them from the dead. It was this encounter with Jesus, alive and enspirited after his death, which brought the Christian faith to birth out of the ruins of the extraordinary movement around Jesus before his death. On this experience of encountering Jesus they based all their new faith and hope. Paul is especially emphatic on this point.

We must think about this extraordinary sequence of events: the collapse of the movement, the execution of Jesus, the psychological effect of which was the death of God, the reappearance of Jesus, the birth of new spiritual vitality of an astonishing kind. This sequence means that, just as Jesus 'buried' God for them, so Jesus made God alive again and was the centre of a new God-consciousness. In other words, the first believers experienced a re-centring of their God-consciousness. Psychologically there was a displacement of divinity from the old God whom guilt kept remote and overpowering, into Jesus. I am convinced that the root of Christianity's subsequently *formulated* belief in the Godhead of Jesus is here, in this first experience of him as 'what it felt like for their God to be alive again, and alive as never before'.

There is a limit to how much large spiritual change the psyche can take; it is impossible to take all at once all the dimensions of such change. The main weight, at the beginning of the new experience of God in Jesus, was carried by 'Jesus newly alive': there was the new divine life. God, the old God once sealed off by guilt and now 'dead', would be temporarily in the shade. That is what I mean by a psychological displacement of divinity from 'God' to Jesus.

Very soon the original God would reappear, and wonderfully so, as the Father who had 'died' in order to cure our envy of his all-powerful life, and was now seen to have declared his love for us by enacting it in bringing Jesus, our representative, into his immortality. The displacement of divinity from 'God' to Jesus would now be experienced as an *extension* of divinity from God into Jesus: God opening up his eternal vitality to us in lifting Jesus out of death to be with him eternally.

The extension of divinity from God to Jesus is bewildering and demands a bridge between these two extremes of infinity and humanness in God. That bridge is the Holy Spirit, the life of the extension of divinity.

This is only a sketch for a new way of appropriating the Christian mystery which later came to be known as Trinity and Incarnation. It requires a great deal more thought, but it already suggests a critique of a new style of theologizing which maintains that in the original Christian belief Jesus was not God but only an exceptional prophet. This view fails to take into account the psychological dimension of Christian beginnings: the traumatic experience of a death of God and the filling of this void by a resurrected man. You couldn't go through the experience of investing everything in that man during his lifetime, of being robbed by him of all your religion, of being reawakened by him as from a profound sleep, and still keep the old God in place, with Jesus as merely one of his prophets. To play down the divinity of Jesus is to undo that traumatic spiritual turning-point in the religious history of humankind. It is to turn back to the twilight that preceded that moment.

It is also to be noted that the old God, the God shadowed by guilt, is much more congenial to the powers which rule this world.

The Jesus revolution threatens those powers, in opening to us a freedom beyond this world. At the Council of Nicaea, at which the Godhead of Jesus was made explicit, the Christian Emperor preferred the opposing view called Arianism. On this view, God would be on top, under him Jesus, under Jesus the Emperor, under the Emperor the people. This desire of worldly power to take over Christianity in interpreting it on its own terms is a huge subject. It doesn't stop when Emperors stop. It is alive and well today. Christianity, in so far as it is alive at all today, is 'counter-cultural'. The cornerstone of this counter-cultural belief is the Godhead of a publicly executed man.

Summary

The awesome encounter with this dead man alive in power caused, in those who experienced it, a psychological displacement of divinity from the old God to the new Man. This massive shift was soon followed by the emergence of the larger pattern, in which the old God becomes new, becomes the Father who shows his care for man by raising him from the dead to be with him forever. Thus displacement of divinity is seen to be in reality extension of divinity. Finally, the prodigious divine vitality that conjoins the infinite mystery with a divine man is experienced, and named the Holy Spirit. With this, the pattern becomes cyclic, a system, a flow of life between Father and Son through the Spirit. The three stages or shock-waves of the Resurrection encounter are thus these: displacement, extension, cyclic life-flow.

This grass-roots derivation of the Trinity depends on the pre-religious understanding of our God-connection. For that understanding, the meaning of 'God' is shaped by a person's psychological state. Thus, while a person is still in guilt, 'God' is to him the jealous, all-dominating one, the threat to man's fragile existence. For the disciples of Jesus, this 'God' dies with the collapse of the Jesus movement. The 'God' they next encounter, the next divine affective focus, is Jesus as a power greater than death. As the meaning of this sinks in, they are able to experience the original God *not* as jealous or domineering but as loving, as bringing us into his own immortal life. Finally, the sense of the sheer vitality of God can burst upon the soul and be named 'Holy Spirit'. Thus the matrix of the images of the divine Persons is 'the infinite connection' as it undergoes the transformation of the encounter with the risen Jesus. The pre-religious concentration of divine energy takes, under the pressure of this encounter, the shape of Father, Son and Spirit. The infinite connection, which always gets a name with religious conversion, gets the three names with this super-conversion.

26. A Disciple Speaks

It is the day after 14th Nisan, and God is dead. There is nothing left of that magic dream which Jesus conjured up and persuaded us to step into with both feet, that dream which became for us the world.

What was the dream? It was not like a dream; it only now looks like a dream. It was not like a dream; on the contrary it was the most real state of mind and feeling we had ever known. We had been schooled from our earliest years to believe in God. This was as though all that we had believed about God were coming true. It was the uncanny feeling of stepping through the ancient words and their images into the thing itself. Those words and their images appeared to us now as the creation of men: in the company of this man they seemed like the discarded toys of an earlier age. Yet nothing was thrown away. It was not a case of believing something different. It was a case of believing more; of believing more because now we saw. All that we had ever believed, our whole past as pious Jews, came miraculously alive; became somehow obvious, for the world itself was transparent over it, the world that once looked so real in its own right before *he* came and we had only the tenaciously-held memories of a people to pit against the harsh facts of existence and political humiliation.

Now all this has gone. Everything has gone. It is not merely the absence of God, an experience known so well to our people and our prophets, but the death of God. For only that God could be experienced as dead who had been experienced, beyond all belief, as living.

It is the day after the day which saw the end. Sleep came to us, the heavy stupid sleep of overwhelming shock and loss. After sleep, refreshed, we experience the world *without* what till recently we had. The world awakes and we with it, empty. There is a settling. The emptiness of the world without God, we now realize, has its own voice, different from the voice of shock and grief. Everyone knows that curious comfort which is in a bereavement, of a weight lifted. However intense the love, the loss is a weight lifted. Indeed, in a strange way, the lightening, the weightless feeling, is more pronounced in a more painful bereavement. There is something of this weightlessness in how we feel today. We cannot live without love, but love demands, and life with the death of the beloved is undemanding. There is a slack relief.

Demands—there are no demands now, none of that continual challenge to be more, to burn more, as veil after veil was pierced and life came into the light. How odd the soul feels without this habitual stretching—as though its spring had gone. It is almost like a revelation—as though there were another side to the soul which all our schooling in God hid from us, an emptiness of which all schooling in God is perforce the denial, however piously it is referred to. Prayer, we now realize with a shock, was a denial of this inner emptiness, and its replacement by guilt. There is no God for the emptiness; for the emptiness is his denial. When people feel it, they feel there is no God. No one will ever know how we feel it today.

A day later

Today it happened. We saw him. Who? O him. I think, in retrospect, that I saw him *with* that emptiness I spoke of, as though the emptiness were a kind of second sight. Yes, it was the virgin soul, never touched by religiousness, that opened puppy eyes to see what we undoubtedly and, at first doubtingly, saw. That strange 'other side of the soul' knew him, and knew him for more than the man we thought we knew. That other side of the soul, that original creature-emptiness which all religious training leaves in the shadows, knows only one thing: its God, its Creator, its origin and life and reason for being. That other side is utterly simple, and with its simplicity we saw Jesus Lord and God. It seems that we spoke better than we knew yesterday when we said 'God is dead!'

Since then, life has consisted in growing in the vision. Not without words—exciting new words which, we know, are changing forever the religious universe. God is this man. This man had come to epitomize finally all our hope and all our emptiness; and when that space became alive God became alive. God is this man in us. We experience God as Father with a genuine shock of paternity, like discovering you're the son of a millionaire! Is that what he was experiencing when we overheard him sometimes at night muttering 'Abba, Abba!'? We have come into this man and feel with his heart and look out through those eyes. God we now know as Spirit, as the heart of that equation between God and life which no religiousness ever quite dares to make for fear of losing all touch with guilt. As we have now! It is all washed away by the blood which now we drink!

27. Displacement of Divinity

Evidence for the 'displacement of divinity' is abundant in the New Testament writings. In the new faith, Jesus figures as much as God. Although the new faith is precisely a new access to God, and readily expresses itself in praise of God, *in* this sense of access and in this praise Jesus is constantly named as a new focus of our primordial religiousness. In the earliest of these 'confessions' or hymns, whether or not they contain a formal statement that Jesus is God, Jesus has divine honours far in excess of what would be permissible to orthodox Jews. Incidentally, this very un-Jewish way of celebrating Jesus affords a kind of proof for the Resurrection: some extraordinary and unprecedented experience rendered these strict monotheists free, and compelled, to celebrate Jesus *with* God as a second focus for this new access to the one God. The common expression 'Jesus is Lord', 'Lord' being the title of God, implies an extension of the title to Jesus. My reason for saying that the first form of this extension was more like a displacement is a combination of the death of God and the vividness of the encounter with Jesus. The life God had lost for them reappeared as Jesus. This displacement of divinity to Jesus remained as the divinity *of* Jesus after the fuller picture had assembled, with God raising Jesus from the dead.

To say that in this first impact Jesus was experienced as 'stronger than death' does not mean survival. It does not mean anything that can be said within the parameters of the present age. It refers to the new age, in which death no longer has the last word. Jesus is the new man inaugurating the new age. This power to innovate on history itself is the power they experienced in him at first as the new place, the displacement, of divinity.

Closely woven into this experience of Jesus as Lord was the experience of the Holy Spirit. This was the other power-centre for the new experience of divinity. In the Holy Spirit there blended the mysterious God of the beginning and the humanness of God as Jesus. What did it mean to experience this dynamic oneness of God and Jesus? It meant that Jesus no longer appeared as an extension of God such that each who experienced him would be confined within himself as one who saw and wondered: Jesus was now experienced as the extension of God in celebrating which the disciples came into a single common consciousness.

We can trace this sense of Jesus as extension of God back to the dark days of the crucifixion. Then God, such as he was, was all tied up with the dead man; the disciples who thus identified God with Jesus remained tragically separated and helplessly bewildered in this contemplation. With the Resurrection, the extension of God into Jesus is a live reality into which they are drawn as into the one Spirit of the living God who raised Jesus from death.

In the tradition the Holy Spirit is the dynamic unity of the Father and the Son. Equally the Holy Spirit is the shared consciousness of the believers. These two main descriptions of the Spirit are functionally one. The life that conjoins heaven and earth is the life in which the believers consciously participate. The ineffable depths of the Spirit conjoining the mystery and the humanness of divinity are the depths in which all who are converted recognize themselves and each other in a transformed world. The ultimate reason why humans do not share a common consciousness is the remoteness of God: for this is the cause, and the effect, of the guilt that keeps us from each other. It is the humanity of God as Jesus which abolishes this remoteness. But for God to be human is not enough. It is necessary that the God who is human is also the God who is infinitely mysterious. Only in *that* understanding are we liberated from our mutually separated existence. Only so can our private struggle with God be common. That understanding, that communication, that 'fellowship', is the Holy Spirit.

28. Behind the Death of God—the Love of God

There is a difference between the death of God as experienced by the disciples during the Good Friday period and as understood once the resurrection encounters have occurred. After Easter, when God is not only alive again but alive for the astonished soul as it were for the first time, the meaning of his having died is understood. It is the behaviour of the lover. Human guilt, since the beginning of human time, has conceived the infinite as infinite power over against human weakness. This is the great projection, the primordial example of that guilt-projection of shadow onto the withdrawn-from other which permeates human society. It is so strong, it enters so deeply into and reshapes the very conviction of God's reality, that only the surrender, the death, the non-self-insistence, of God himself can break it.

At that crucial moment when human psychology is floundering in a new and bewildering experience of God's *weakness,* infinite love capitalizes on that experience and confirms it as an encounter with himself as the surrendering lover. Only after the resurrection can this death of God be understood as the act of the lover. Only before the resurrection can this death of God find its point of entry into the soul. The bewilderment of Golgotha is its necessary climate. No instruction, no intuition, no vision even, can dislodge guilt from its central position in the human soul, whence it directs the soul's perception of God. Nothing short of the catastrophe can do that. When the catastrophe has done its work and left the soul in pieces, no longer holding itself together under the dreaded infinite power, then at last the Absolute can be encountered not as power but as love: the Absolute encountered as love, not by any equation that the mind or heart of man could conceivably dream up, not in thought, but in the psyche. The immemorial human psyche, home of eros, of guilt and of all the marvellous and conflicting movements shaped by those two forces, encountered the Absolute as love. The shock waves of that explosion are to be felt on any page of the New Testament.

The infinite power that guilt saw as withholding eternal life from the hands of grasping man reveals itself as the infinite love who invites man into eternal friendship. Infinite love is seen doing this in Jesus who, representing all humanity, is raised into the eternal friendship of God.

The first experience of God as love is the risen Jesus, the recipient of that love. Yet the encounter with the risen Jesus involved, at first, a displacement of divinity from God to Jesus. Is there a contradiction here? No, in that first vital moment the mystery of Jesus is established in power. Jesus is humanity's first sight of who God really is, after God as humanity saw him has died. It is from Jesus that the disciples derived the eternal life they saw in him. Only God can give eternal life, only God can make us his friends. Jesus is the Lord. Only when that is secure, only when this strange new bridgehead of divinity has been acknowledged by the bewildered and blissful soul of the disciple, the Father can and must appear, his love manifest in the raising of Jesus. So at the very beginning the foundation of faith is laid. In the very first experience, it is known that Jesus has what he has for us not as an adopted or chosen one, not as an exceptionally faithful one, not as the first of a series, but as a mysterious extension of God. Only as such could he have eternal life *for us*.

The Church has held onto that basic logic, sometimes by the skin of her teeth, as at Nicaea. The bottom line of Nicaea was that Jesus had done for us what only God could do, had given us what only God could give, and therefore had to be God, whatever the awesome problems created by such an equation in the intellectual world. The same argument was used to establish the divinity of the Holy Spirit. A profound spiritual instinct directs the tradition here, a deep human pessimism which knows that no human example can break the chain of guilt. This instinct remembers Golgotha and its despair, which only God himself could lift, so that he who lifted it was, and is eternally, God.

29. John's World

In the last chapter it was said that the immemorial human psyche, home of eros and of guilt, encountered the Absolute as love. This encounter is the origin of the Christian sense of the fundamental oneness between love for God and love for our neighbour, of which the quintessential description is perhaps the first letter of John. All the world religions intuit this unity. Christianity has its own special sense of it.

The Christian's love for his neighbour derives, we have always been taught, from his love for God. This love, in its turn, is the response to *God's* love for *him*. This is why Christian love is able to extend beyond the ties of family and friends, even to the enemy and, even beyond the enemy, to the active persecutor.

This Christian love, which extends to the neighbour whoever he may be, has seldom been understood to have quite that spontaneity and immediacy of feeling which exists among friends. The reason for this, surely, is that few Christians experience that equation of God with love which transforms the psyche, liberating eros from guilt, its close companion, with the embrace of the love that God is: *agape*. When the psyche, in all its complexity, begins to sense the ultimate mystery as love and not as power, everything changes. The guilt and anxiety in every person's link with the mystery which constitutes us is being dispelled. Habitual channellings of eros cease to be the only channels. The stab of compassion and tenderness is no longer confined to the cultivated areas of love, but may occur anywhere. This is the Christian experience, which is, indistinguishably, the recognition of God as love and the recognition of Jesus as God. It is the resurrection experience.

To recognize Jesus as God is to have effective in myself that presence of God as love, not power, which, dissolving guilt at its core, releases in me the love of which the new community is constituted. Thus is verified the prayer in John's gospel 'that they may be one, as you, Father, and I are one'. The oneness of the Father and Jesus, experienced in the resurrection encounter as the divine love, supplants divine power, releases people, delivers them into mutual love in community. The principle of this mutual love in community is the Holy Spirit, not surprisingly, because the Holy Spirit is the very personality of that oneness of Father and Son which, experienced, releases people into community. In short, the dynamic of the divine persons in the new life takes on a new coherence once we centre it on the encounter with the risen Jesus in its full context, namely the story of his disciples. All that is said in the New Testament about the bestowal of God's love on us 'in Christ Jesus our Lord' needs to be heard today with a new understanding of the receiver as one who pre-religiously desires God's affirming word. In this respect, our theology has been dumb, and in the realm of the spirit dumbness soon becomes deafness.

'Let us love one another, because love comes from God. Whoever loves is a child of God and knows God. Whoever does not love does not know God, because God is love' (1 John 4:7-9). This author is talking about love as an indivisible reality that is God, that is of God, and that is between those who love. He is virtually inverting 'God is love' into 'love is God', while continuing to maintain the first proposition. This inversion is regularly made by romantics, who presume the presence of God (in which they are not really too interested) in 'the holiness of the heart's affections' (in which they are passionately interested).

Our author is able to make the inversion, and to have it both ways, within the Christian context of faith and the awesomeness of God and salvation through the blood of Christ, because he knows that primary resurrection experience of God as love in which the psyche is totally transformed. Knowing God as love means knowing love as God. Not only is the author's freedom with the concept of love within the Christian context, it is much more controlled by that context than are most Christian statements about love. The average Christian statement on love, not being made under the compulsion of the Resurrection, does not feel that presence of God in everything which the resurrection experience releases. It therefore feels it has to be careful in what it says, and so ends in moralism.

30. Nicaea and Afterwards

The divinity of Jesus originally meant heaven on earth as an experience. It meant Jesus calling out into total freedom that feeling for God which is not otherwise free. Jesus drew into himself the soul's secret sense of who God is, which guilt will not let it utter. He was the focus of that sense. That is the meaning of 'Jesus is Lord'. It was the cry of a free people, that is, of a people who had found themselves in the God from whom human life is alienated. The humanity of God was the filling of a vacuum whose enormousness could only be understood after it was filled: the amazing capacity of the human creature to be empty of God. That emptiness, man's extraordinary capacity to be somehow apart from God, was brought to its critical point during those hours when 'God was dead'. What filled it could only be God. Jesus filled it. Jesus *is* God. All the experience of the Jesus mission and its traumatic end was involved and invoked by the first people to cry out: 'Jesus is Lord'.

We have not even yet realized how much our way of conceiving of God's transcendence is shaped by the deep guilt which screens him off from us. The humanity of God is the vision which clears before our uncomprehending eyes as guilt is taken away, just as a sudden shift of the near cloud will reveal to the mountain-climber the glorious scene. The Lamb of God takes away the sin of the world. He appears in sin's sudden absence.

The new people who ran around saying 'Jesus is Lord' were giving expression to a new religious consciousness, an awareness of God without guilt. God was no longer culture's 'God': he had 'come out' from the corner of the soul where guilt locks him up; he was human, physical. But he didn't stop being mysterious, ultimate. To the consciousness of God as both mysterious and human at the same time they gave a special name. It was the experience of the Holy Spirit, a super-consciousness in which everything came together and all people came together.

However difficult it is for us to get into, that experience is the only way of knowing what the divinity of Jesus means. I do not know what it means by simply thinking of 'God', then thinking of 'Jesus' and saying they are one. Such a knowing is purely verbal. The attribution of divinity to Jesus comes from the deepest reaches of human consciousness when the love therein has been set free from guilt. Of this new liberated God-connection, Jesus is the focus. That is why 'Jesus is Lord' is the rallying-cry, the 'logo', of the liberated. 'Jesus is Lord' is the expression of a consciousness of God as purely generous and life-giving, a consciousness of God as ultimate yet not 'Master', a consciousness of God as love and nothing else.

This new consciousness becomes articulate in two complementary ways. If I ask what it says about human beings, the answer is 'Jesus is God', meaning that our life is raised out of guilt into emotional equality with God. If I ask what it says about God, the answer is: 'God is loving Father, beloved Son, these two one in Holy Spirit'. This is the origin of the two central Christian doctrines, of Incarnation and Trinity.

In the three Councils, of Nicaea (325), Ephesus (431) and Chalcedon (451), the Church worked through the logical problems created by this beyond-logical belief. Nicaea accepted the logical conclusion of the fact that Jesus did for us what only God can do, that is, make us friends of God. One who does what only God can do must be God, whatever the appearances to the contrary, i.e., the human limitations of Jesus. Ephesus met to settle a big row which started when a preacher said you obviously couldn't call Mary 'the Mother of God', the idea was preposterous. The Council decided that you could and should and indeed must call Mary the Mother of God; for a mother begets not 'humanity' but 'a man', and the man, the person, Jesus, *was* God, as Nicaea had already affirmed. Here a distinction emerges which will prove of crucial importance at the next Council: between 'nature' and 'person', between 'humanity' and 'a man'. Chalcedon used this distinction to show how Jesus could logically be both God and man: he was one person in two natures, divine and human.

What was forgotten, and what Christology must remember, is that the formulation that Jesus is 'one person in two natures' depends upon, is the intellectual recognition of, the original psychologically and spiritually revolutionary experience. It is only for a person who shares that experience that Jesus *is* the God and man affirmed by the formula. To say that the formula is a triumph of faith is easily misunderstood, for it does not ask a blind assent to itself in all its apparent impossibility. Rather, it represents the acceptance, in our critical yes-or-no intelligence, of that transformation of the heart which took place when the executed Jesus returned to his own in the Spirit, and when he now comes to his own in the Spirit. In this sense the formula is indeed a triumph of faith.

Christianity is weighed down by a divine-human Jesus who, instead of being recognizable by the human spirit as its liberation from guilt and all evil and unfreedom, is imposed on the human spirit from the outside. I do not know any theologian who has asked: What psychological transformation is happening when a person affirms Jesus as God? Of what inner change is that belief the expression? Believers seem to think that Jesus is safer in a formula than in people's minds and hearts, in their self-awareness.

31. A Celebration

This book is for me a celebration. It celebrates the very inward event of my becoming able to detach the meaning of Christianity's central belief, that Jesus is God, from the correct and indispensable conceptual structure in which the first church councils expressed it. This has taken me sixty years.

I was so habituated to understanding the divinity of Jesus as the content of this technical language that I didn't even recognize what I was doing, rather as a paralysed limb will become an unnoticed part of one's system, until one experiences the ache and awkwardness of recovery. The first attempt to move the limb involved the creation of a brash, very physical image of 'displacement'. How exhilarating it was when I allowed that image to come! It was my definitive break with the hallowed words for this matter, which come with fatal ease to the theologian's pen. Those words, used in answer to the real questions which the psyche today puts to Christianity, are killers. They state the intention *not* to answer the real questions, which are: What is this truth, that a man is God? What does it do in the soul? Of what transformation within the soul is it the expression? How does it liberate? What does it liberate? What difference does it make?

I am aware that answers to all these questions can be given with the Nicene formula as base: true answers about the newly revealed dignity of man and so forth. We are so deeply ensconced temporally on this side of the formula, which is in this respect like the temporal Chinese Wall to which Eliot once compared the poetry of Milton, that it is not easy to formulate a question about the divinity of Jesus which could not be answered in such ways. The only way to reach that question which has worked for me is to ask: 'How did they first know? What was the first knowing?' The advantage of this approach is that it forces us to consider a knowing that Jesus was God, previous to which the idea of a man being God was either

97

blasphemous or idolatrous or nonsensical. None of those under-
standings of the equation would be correct. No conceivable understanding of the equation apart from the experience in which it was
forged and impressed on the soul would be correct.

The proposition 'Jesus is God' depends for its meaning, not only
for its truth, on the unique process through which certain persons
went to come into its daylight. In other words, the divinity of Jesus
is a truth more shaped by the way it came and comes to be known
than are other truths.

How could it be otherwise? How could the terrible proportions
of God's love be for the newspapers? How could they be crystal-
lized in a formula without that formula being dangerous and
sending us to the saint and the prophet, and above all to prayer,
for its understanding and use? How could the original wellspring
of its provenance not be privileged, be an integral part of itself?

That provenance is not simply an insight or a vision. It is not
like Mohammed's experience in the cave, whence came the huge
visionary idea of 'Islam', submission to God. The confession that
Jesus is Lord was the culmination of a process, a dramatic revelatory process. The interaction of Jesus with his disciples produced a
unique effect in them because of the unique person Jesus was; this
effect, this divine transformation of the world in which they lived,
interacted with the way the world is to produce a unique crisis, an
experienced emptiness of the soul which only God could fill. Jesus
was experienced, after his death, as filling it; Jesus, then, was God.
The godhead of Jesus is inscribed in those events and emerges from
their process, as a photographic image comes to stand out from the
film as it floats in the developing fluid. This simile has a curious
aptness since 1898, when Secondo Pia saw the first film to be exposed to the Shroud of Turin yielding to chemistry the shroud's
millennial secret.

We only know the meaning of the divinity of Jesus in so far as
we are somehow in touch with how God showed people that Jesus
was divine. 'No one can say "Jesus is Lord" but in the Holy Spirit.'
The word 'This is my beloved son' describes the *way* in which this
truth is understood and known. It is a truth received from critical
events coming to a climax which could only be divinely revelatory.
That is its shape and meaning.

Until the divinity of Jesus is recovered in its first and continuing
springing upon the Christian soul, there are serious embarrass-

ments in the Christian mind. The worst is that the area of Jesus' divinity, being ruled by the conciliar formulas with which the divinity has become identified, will be avoided. Shunning abstraction, the theologian and preacher will seek more promising pastures. What he thus turns his back on, or vaguely files, is the love and healing of God at its maximum intensity. I never spoke of the divinity of Jesus. I regarded it as 'in some sense true but not for now'. It is only the essence of Christianity!

As well as avoidance, there is the attempt to tame this area, to reduce its power to embarrass. This is done by virtually identifying the divinity of Christ with its credal formulation, stressing the Hellenistic, non-scriptural climate of the formula, and then producing, in contrast with the climate and with its divine Christ, a sensitive New Testament exegesis. Even when the historical unsatisfactoriness of this procedure has been demonstrated, suspicion remains. The heart is not in a 'high Christology', because we have not discovered the role of the heart in producing a high Christology. That is the crux. That's what this book is all about.

On the other side, on the side of the 'orthodox' response to the modernizers, the same fundamental imbalance is perceivable. From this camp come condemnations, accusations and every sort of rhetoric; this is how people behave when they are fighting for a concept, a slogan, an abstraction. For the 'orthodox', as well as for the modernizers, that is the sort of thing the divinity of Jesus is.

Lonergan's definition of theology would imply that culture is, or at least can be, the exacerbation of the problem of belief: 'A theology mediates between a cultural matrix and the significance and role of a religion in that matrix.' The contemporary problematic around the divinity of Jesus certainly illustrates this. We have not drawn upon our culture to the point of deriving categories in terms of which the divine nature of a man could be conceived of as springing itself upon his followers: categories of the lyrical, the romantic (the 'Galilean springtime'), the desolation of the soul, the death of God, an ultimate inconsolability (meaning a state which, if consoled, can only have been consoled by the Ultimate), the place of guilt in a relationship with the Absolute. These very modern categories furnished by our culture need to be organized, rooted in universal anthropology, and then trained onto those crucial days which saw the birth of Christianity.

In default of even the realization that some such operation is required, the divinity of Jesus stands before us in its clear conciliar formulation as that which is to be believed, and as that which people find unbelievable, in other words as the test of faith, instead of being an indispensable logical note to a belief whose substance is an experience of the risen Jesus in the Spirit.

It is frequently said that the conciliar Christology spoke to the needs of a now-past culture, that it is time we got beyond Chalcedon. There is some truth in this, but it tends to confuse the issue. I am not asserting an inability of the conciliar Christology to speak to our time, but an inability of the conciliar Christology by itself to convey the substance of the Incarnation to our time or to any other time, including the time of the Councils themselves.

Just as these Christological formulas are inefficacious by themselves for any age, so, understood in their true, clarifying function, they are applicable and mandatory for believers of any age. To any believer who considers them, whether in the fifth century or in the twenty-fifth, they are reminding him of the stark exigencies of his belief in Jesus when brought to the bar of logic. They are saying to him: however you have come to this belief, in however deep a sense of mystery it plunges you, however unspeakable the experienced essence of it may be, you must realize that the difference between creature and Creator is infinite, that there are no gradations across that gap, and you must say on which side of that gap is this person you believe in. Whatever forms a future Christology may take, it will always draw to itself this logical explicator, this reminder of the infinite difference and of the attendant either-or.

I suspect that some of the talk of 'getting beyond Chalcedon' is unconsciously motivated by a desire to disembarrass Christology of this reminder. If we think of the early Councils only as products of a past culture, we can get them out of the way of our theologizing. This means silencing that tiresome logical voice which says: 'Which is it to be, finite or infinite?' Why do we want to silence that voice? Because we lack a way of thinking of the divinity of Jesus which is independent of that voice and so has nothing to fear from it. This has been my experience. I am only returning to the conciliar Christology now that the divinity of Jesus has found a home in my thinking independently of that Christology.

I also remember being very emphatic that the conciliar formulas do not give us a psychology of Jesus as God and Man. You can't think of Jesus switching back and forth between his divine and his human nature. Correct. But it never occurred to me to go on to ask: 'What does give us a psychology of Jesus God and Man, or rather, as it has turned out, a psychology/anthropology/sociology of Jesus God and Man?'

Only with the coming of a way of thinking of Jesus' divinity independent of the logical voice can I see clearly that the distinction between creature and Creator, on which Athanasius, the principal architect of Nicaea, was very clear, is not relative to a particular culture. If that distinction is no longer relevant to Christology, what on earth is Christology?

Perhaps the Quest for the Historical Jesus was at least in part motivated by the *believer's* need to have some intellectual point of reference, some meaning-giving context, for the object of his belief other than the structure provided by the conciliar formulas. I do not believe the quest can be wholly accounted for by the positivism which so drearily directed it. I can recognize in retrospect that it was such a need which got me slogging through Schweitzer and others. I did not then realize how much, much more would have to be done before my real Christological need could clarify itself, in the way a need does when we experience some satisfaction of it.

I feel a considerable sympathy for Alfred Loisy, who stumbled on the area which an existential Christology can be, and has to be, elaborated. As the area was new, he made some serious confusions, thinking he was being purely critical when he was also being philosophical. He was in addition an impulsive and opinionated man. But the Church authorities, at least in hindsight, were so heavily invested in a dogmatic Christology as the only possibility that they would not have known what I am talking about. Loisy must, as a result, have felt he had entered a forbidden and exciting area. He heard Authority saying: 'You are not to go in there!' Perhaps his unconscious heard their unconscious saying, under its breath, 'because God knows what you'll find!' What Loisy 'found' was 'a village craftsman, naive and enthusiastic, who believes the end of the world near at hand, believes in the establishment of a Kingdom of Justice, in the advent of God on earth, and who, firmly set in this first illusion, assumes the principal role in the organization of the unrealizable city.'[1] Loisy's eventual abandonment of all supernat-

---

[1] Francesco Turvasi, *The Condemnation of Alfred Loisy and the Historical Method.* (Rome: Edizioni di Storia e Letteratura, 1979).

ural religion was assuredly a personal option in the crucial area of belief and unbelief, but its stormy prelude illustrates what Lonergan means by a crisis of culture rather than of faith. The former crisis easily turns into the latter in an individual. As David Jones has said: 'It is easy to miss him at the turn of a civilization.'

32. Is Christ God?

We must now consider a rather tempting way of accounting for the Christian belief in the divinity of Jesus, which goes like this.

After the death of their leader, the disciples of Jesus came to see in him the Christ, the King-Messiah, the anointed one of God. There had taken place, it seems, in the period immediately previous to Jesus, a blending of two traditional images, of the King-Messiah and of the Son of Man, that mysterious figure whom Daniel saw in his vision, coming upon the clouds of heaven. The matter is very complicated and, as the reader will have realized by now, not my field. What concerns us here is that neither the Messiah nor the Son of Man nor a blending of the two could possibly be regarded as divine, as the equal of God. It was as the incarnation of that mysterious mythic personage, and not as divine, that the first believers saw their hero.

Very soon the new sect started preaching to and interacting with the pagan world. In that preaching they called their hero *Kurios,* Lord. In the pagan world, there were plenty of lords and gods. There was nothing there of the ruthless spiritual purity of Jewish monotheism, but the new sect were passionate believers in *their* Lord. There could be no question of enthroning him among the existing lords, or adding his name to the honourable list. He was above them all. He was the Lord of lords, the King of kings. Who can he be to whom our allegiance is due beyond all the authorities that confront us in this life? Who but God?

Thus, by a rather fascinating process, Jesus acquires divine status. The process is a dual one. First, the pagan culture permits the giving of divine honours to a man, and this permission is tacitly accepted. Second, within the ambit of this permission, Jesus was raised above all the Dominions and Powers and so acquired that divine status which believers in the one God accord only to the power to which alone the conscience is subject. The Jewish milieu does not allow divine status to Jesus, so there is a sidestep into the pagan world which allows divine status to all sort of people. From thence Jesus ascends to the level of God, of the God, be it noted, whom some serious pagans regarded as sovereign and one. Jesus joined the Hall of Fame and, once there, made it to the top.

This idea is fairly old but has reappeared recently in a book by a group of English theologians called *The Myth of God Incarnate*.[2] It has appeared in many forms, all of which I leave to the Christian apologist. As an account of the linguistic fortunes of the new sect this opinion seems acceptable. There was no way, within the Jewish tradition, of saying that Jesus was the equal of God. There was a way, at least towards saying this, in the Greco-Roman world. Perhaps the new believers put Jesus as high as they could within their tradition, which was King-Messiah-Son-of-Man; once they got him outside that tradition the lid was off and Jesus could go up all the way.

The capital question is: In what sense did they regard 'the Christ' as the best name they could give Jesus? Was it the best available, or was it quite simply the best, the most suited to their experience of him? Many would call this a non-question. They would say that people can only, and only want to, think in the categories provided by their culture. Yet this view does not account for those moments of creative unrest when a new, unformulable thought is trying to break through: the anguish of an Einstein, for instance, about whom top physicists say they cannot see how he managed to think up his universe. Did the disciples of Jesus find themselves in that kind of interim, in this case a religio-cultural interim, as a result of a unique experience, doing what they could with existing religious images, yet knowing they were into something totally new and unprecedented? Do they not show they were in such an interim by the things they attributed to Jesus? He was the Christ, they said, and Christ does not mean God or the equal of God; but he was a Christ who had done for them what only God can do: made them friends of God, given them the Holy Spirit, forgiven all their sins. Their tradition had no name for a human being who could do such things. They gave him the best name the tradition had, and changed forever its meaning by what they believed its new possessor did for them and for all humankind.

[2] John Hick, ed., *The Myth of God Incarnate* (London: S.C.M. Press).

My main concern is to look hard at that in which the proponents of an evolved divinity of Jesus seem not to be at all interested, namely the experience of the disciples. What that experience may have been plays no part in the theory: it suffices that they 'came to realize' or 'came to believe' that Jesus was the promised Messiah. Some sort of combination—and gradual please!—of grief lifting, memory awakening, and hope returning, will suffice to provide the first stage in the fortunes of our doctrine. This contentment with vagueness is extraordinary, for religious experience is a fascinating and variegated subject, as William James discovered. How very strange to feel no need to posit some profound and unique experience in those who originated the most influential, and the only universal, of the world religions! This agnosticism, reverent and otherwise, is extended to the experience of Jesus himself. No one hesitates to accord to Mohammed the status of great creative visionary; but when it comes to Jesus and his movement, he is just someone whom some people came to think of as God. Somehow the initiative for this enormous religious innovation falls between Jesus and his first promoters. Can anything so vigorous as Christianity have got off to such a muddled start, being told by the surrounding culture, in its two earliest cultural habitats, what it believed about its Founder? There is a heavy improbability here, which it is the apologist's role to highlight.

I am vitally interested in going beyond the limit the apologist rightly sets himself. I must now state my parameters. First, I believe what the Council of Nicaea said about Jesus: that he is one in being with the Father. Second, I do not see how that belief can be said to be true if it does not represent what was in substance believed from the very beginning of the Christian preaching. Of course it could have been believed from the beginning and still not be true. I am only concerned here to state that if it was not believed from the beginning it *cannot* be true.

These parameters compel me to try to envisage a way in which the sense of the divine agency of Jesus arose. The attempt to do this involves me in a most searching analysis of religious experience: the area, be it remembered, where the proponents of the opinion under review evince little interest. The experience I invoke is a unique form of the dark night of the soul. It is that sense of the death of God which the execution of Jesus created. If Jesus was the man without sin, as the Christian tradition has believed him to be from its beginning, the sense of the reality of God that he evoked in the people close to him was something beyond our capacity to imagine, for none of us has ever been touched by a sinless person. Of course this conclusion, also, depends on faith, which is one of my parameters. Correspondingly, the sense of the death of God which the failure and execution of Jesus caused was something beyond our capacity to imagine.

The mystics who deal with the deeper religious desolation insist that the condition is inconsolable. The soul has invested too much of its natural resources beyond the realm of nature for any revival in that realm to afford consolation for the total loss which seems to have happened in the world beyond. St John of the Cross, and many others, are clear here: 'no pleasure in God, or in anything else'. Eliot has some haunting descriptions in *The Family Reunion:* 'The unexpected crash of the iron cataract.' 'You do not know what hope is until you have lost it.'

Nothing can console this condition except the return of God. So anything which does console this condition must be the return of God. The condition cannot be consoled either by a return of natural contentment or by such a return masquerading as the return of God. Consolation, when it comes, is what Ignatius called 'consolation without a cause'. This is one of the principal ways in which the presence of God is known, in which a new lifting of the soul is known to be of God: when a previous period of severe God-deprivation has made it impossible for this lifting of the soul to be anything else than a touch of God.

The disciples seem to have been positively inundated with consolation. They attributed this to an encounter with Jesus. In their experience, then, Jesus was the finger of God, the very touch of God returning and flooding their world with his Spirit. Jesus was the presence of God in their midst. Jesus the man was doing for their disconsolate soul what only God can do and what, when it happens, is known to be of God.

Surely something like this is the source for the disciples' conviction that God had raised Jesus from death. The experience of the encounter with Jesus as the return of God puts God at the centre of the picture with or in Jesus. Nor is there the opposition scholars sometimes make between the primitive 'God raised Jesus' formula and the later 'Jesus rose'. There is only opposition here when the deeper perspective which underpins both ways of talking has been

106

lost to view. Scholars tend to forget, as they piece together the different formulas, that the first believers did not piece them together the way scholars do. They were excited, even wild, in response to an experience. The theologian is not an antiquary but a detective. He is investigating the most controversial and consequence-laden murder in history. What is the use of a detective who does not identify imaginatively with the odd ways people behave when they are in the throes of deep emotion?

In the mystical perspective I am trying to open up, a total spiritual transformation is happening, of which God and Jesus and the Spirit constitute the centre. The first witnesses believed Jesus to be, in effect, God, because God told them, because they 'heard' it, 'received' it, from God, in a unique instance of the one tested way in which people can know they are hearing from God. Once this is said it becomes even more clear that the divinity of Jesus is something which can *only* be known from God. 'No one says "Jesus is Lord" but in the Holy Spirit', as Paul says (1 Cor. 12:3). A thoughtful unbeliever recognizes that Christianity is a world religion based on an alleged revelation, an alleged contact with the divine. It is only a peculiar combination of cultural familiarity with Christianity and agnosticism which is content to think of Christian origins in terms of a bunch of disciples playing around with images and ideas.

Yet is it not far-fetched to suggest that 'those rough men' (how rough were they, incidentally, minus the gospel movies?) went through an advanced form of the dark night of the soul? That really depends on what you think of Jesus. If you see in him that unique phenomenon, a sinless person, it becomes clear that his effect on his disciples, in building them up and casting them down, breaks the scales of spiritual assessment. Far from furnishing an exaggerated idea of their condition, the Dark Night appears as the best analogue but still far short.

One very important respect in which the desolation of the disciples goes beyond anything described in *The Dark Night of the Soul* is that it was a socialized, shared, common desolation. A shared world had collapsed. A shared God had died. A shared visionary world is more real than a private visionary world, much closer to being believable-in as *the* world, its God more believable-in as who God is for all. Nor would the sharedness of the desolation mitigate it. On the contrary, whatever mutual support there was

107

would be part of the no-longer-consoling natural world of the God-abandoned.

In the above most serious sense, I believe God told the disciples that Jesus was God. I believe that human consciousness was carried over the bottomless chasm that divides the created from the uncreated. I believe it is in consequence a different sort of world. Within this different sort of world, I believe God told the Council of Nicaea that *homoousion* (of the same substance) was the word. Or, to play the game according to the rules, and not to confuse infallibility with inspiration, I believe he headed the Council off *homoiousion* (of like substance). This is what I understand by faith. I cannot pretend I have understood it this way for long.

In my view it is impossible to see that the conciliar formula means what it says and is true, until one has emotionally crossed the divide between our own human world and God's human world. Until that happens, Jesus remains emotionally at the level of the challenge, of question to us, not mediating Godhead except as a catalyst, on the analogy of a Martin Luther King. The divinity-formula is thus taken to be a 'merely logical' way of referring to this radically inadequate conception of the original experience. By a mischievous irony which perpetuates the confusion the formula is described as 'inadequate', whereas the real problem is the lack of an experience adequate to the formula.

To sum up, there are three levels to the critique of that view of Christian beginnings with which this chapter began. At the first level, the glaring omission in this view is highlighted, namely its lack of concern with the religious experience of the disciples. The anomaly of a new faith learning its central belief from the two cultures, Jewish and Greco-Roman, with which it successively interacted, would be pointed out. This is the apologetic level. At the next level we would amplify exegetically the proposition that the risen Jesus was worshipped, and was credited with operations which only God can perform, while it is perfectly true that 'Christ' does not mean the equal of God. The third level is much deeper and more hazardous. It is the level at which this book is written. I have dared to surmise how the human psyche, at the beginning of our era, was shocked into a bliss of which God alone could be the author and from which, thank God, it will never recover.

33. Intellect and Heart

There is always the temptation to think one has the solution to the ills of an epoch, which in this context can be described as our theological disarray, the fracturing of the image of Christ, the polarizations, the multiple positions which rarely make clear their basic assumptions. There is no easy solution, but it is not difficult to name the general cultural *malaise* from which all these ills flow: a deep divide between the intelligence and the heart. The continual and complex interaction between these two centres of thought, which is as essential to healthy spiritual functioning as the circulation of the blood to physical well-being, is dammed up in all sorts of ways. To be more precise, there is a tendency for feelings, attitudes, values to canonize themselves, to generate their own justification and to distrust our good friend intelligence who would question them, sometimes disconcertingly but overwhelmingly to their profit and advancement.

The world of religion is rich in images and symbols, in myths and other forms of story. These are the very stuff of religion, its language, which is a language of the heart. But man does not live by images alone. He desires to know. He hankers for what is absolutely the case. The vitality and flexibility of the images which turn him on spiritually depend on their openness to the question of truth. When, for instance, a theologian previous to Nicaea would say: 'The Son proceeds from the Father as brightness from the sun', the power of this image lay in the realization of faith that it was pointing to something ineffable which cannot be imagined at all.

A serious distortion enters theology when the theologian concentrates on images and their meaning, on words and their connotations, to the exclusion of the question of truth. The Christological theory criticized in the previous chapter is case in point. The theory fixes on the words, especially the names, used by the Christian preaching in its two earliest stages, Jewish and Greco-Roman. It

109

considers carefully the use and associations of those words in those two cultures. It concludes that the preaching, in using those names, King-Messiah, Son of Man, Lord (Kurios) and so forth, meant by them only what those names evoked.

This is to ignore a very simple principle which ordinary people apply daily without noticing it: a thing or a person is known not by what it looks like or feels like, nor by what its name sounds like or evokes, but *by what it does,* by how it behaves, by how it relates to the world. This principle proved crucial in the early centuries of Christianity, when the faith which exploded into consciousness at the encounter with the risen Jesus and the inundation of the Spirit as consolation and peace was calling upon a friendly intelligence to become a coherent belief.

Jesus was the Christ, and 'the Christ' did not for Jews mean the equal of God; but *this* Christ did things for us that only God can do. Thus was he known and honoured as the equal of God. Later the principle took a new form: the Son comes from the Father, and 'comes from' suggests dependence and subordination; but *this* Son does all the things the Father does except generate the Son, is all the things the Father is except 'Father', so he is 'one in being with the Father', as our creed says. Again: the Holy Spirit comes from the Father and the Son, he is 'breathed forth'. Surely the breath depends on and is less than the breather. Even at the more spiritual level, who ever heard of the spirit Gandhi breathed into India as being the equal of Gandhi? But *this* Spirit makes us holy, transforms us, divinizes us, and this only God himself can do. Therefore the Holy Spirit is God.

The doctrine of the Holy Trinity, which focuses the whole Christian belief, was able to be coherently formulated only through an open communication between the multiple images of Scripture (images of father, son and spirit) and the intelligence which reminds us that we know things by their behaviour. The doctrine of the Trinity is the emblem of the marriage of intellect and heart, which God has made and man may not put asunder.

The recognition of this marriage is perhaps the chief glory of the Catholic theological tradition, although that tradition has many sins to its name, high on the list being an irresponsibility to history: the refusal, for instance, to pay attention for nearly two centuries to the problem of the historical Jesus.

In this urgent question of Jesus Christ, once the intellect has had its say and insisted that he is known by what he does, it is for the heart in the last resort to say what he does. Here too the theory under criticism fails us, for it does not inquire into the disciples' experience of the transformation he effected in them. The capacity to fail both in objectivity and in subjectivity is the mark of a captive mind.

Theologians tend these days to talk of a 'high Christology' and a 'low Christology'. If by a 'low Christology' is meant the opinion that the Council of Nicaea, in identifying Jesus ontologically with God, made Jesus to be more than he was, then 'low' is a misleading description. High and low refer to degrees, and there are no degrees between 'Jesus is God' and 'Jesus is not God'. The difference is infinite, and the infinite cannot be calibrated. A low Christology is a 'no' Christology. A high Christology is a 'yes' Christology.

34. Mary—the Catholic Snag?

My Christology is based on the traditional belief that Jesus was sinless. Interpreting this as meaning a freedom from the universal original disaffection with existence and its cause, I find this freedom the central idea for understanding Jesus and the role he played and plays. I run into a difficulty here, for according to the Catholic tradition, Jesus is not the only sinless human being. This status is accorded also to Mary. Now if Jesus is not the only sinless one, he is not only the sinless one. Something more has to be said of him. That something, and not sinlessness, will render him unique and account for his saving power. After all, any Christian would say that Jesus saves us not by being sinless but by being God as well as man.

The sinlessness of Jesus is unique in that *it alone* was brought into the final conflict with the power of sin. It was only in the conflict between Jesus and the forces of this world that the disciples had to face the ultimate crisis of the soul, the death of God which dissolves the master-slave relationship and leaves a void. That void is filled by Jesus newly and bewilderingly alive: alive in a way for which there is no category and in which life's ultimate value and meaningfulness are not shadowed and questioned by death.

What was the source of the divine status of Jesus? It was that he proved stronger than the death to which God, it seemed, had succumbed. His 'thing' came to nothing, his 'God' proved powerless before the banal force of this world, yet here he was! Thus the disciples saw that his intimacy with God, his emotional equality with God, his freedom from the original guilt, was a reality stronger than the death which seemed to have rendered it a mere aspiration or a dream. The sinlessness of Jesus was experienced as triumphant, in a new dimension where it came through as the salient feature, unique in its 'coming through', in being able to appear in power as the centre of a divine displacement. With the

112

reappearance of the original God as lover of humankind in raising Jesus from death, and the realization of the Holy Spirit as spanning the beginningness and the humanness of God, the revelatory process is complete.

Only a Christology of freedom-from-guilt can say what 'came through' the dark days, what 'attracted' divinity into itself by displacement, what appeared as the beloved of God for all of us. Further, only a Christology of sinlessness can appeal for its intelligibility to the whole existential anthropology of original guilt. Only such a Christology can say what has awakened us, and from what we have been awakened.

In engaging with the power of death to make it ineffective the guiltlessness of Jesus has come through to us and brought us into itself. The conquest of evil was not asked of the Virgin Mary's sinlessness.

An even more decisive consideration is that Jesus' emotional equality with God came through death and was communicated to the disciples. It was as communicated by him at the Resurrection that this equality was known by them as triumphant over this world of death. In simpler words, he gave his friendship with God to them. But only God can make people his friends. Therefore Jesus, in making the disciples friends of God, gave them what only God can give. He who does what only God can do is God. Thus Jesus' emotional equality with God, as something he could give to others, as communicable, presupposes an ontological equality with God. It is as communicable that Jesus' emotional equality with God belongs to one who must be said to be God.

In contrast, Mary's sinlessness is not something given to others but received. Do not all the redeemed receive the guiltlessness of Jesus? What is special about Mary? Here we meet a category which seems to have been instinctively arrived at, and which had immense importance in patristic theology: the category of the perfect recipient. The Fathers envisaged the salvation process as involving: humanity as active (in Jesus), humanity as sinful-receptive (in people as sinners), and humanity as perfectly receptive (in Mary, and in the Church). This Mary-Church image is nowadays totally neglected and must be retrieved. Among theologians one seldom hears anything sensible about the Church, and never anything about the Virgin Mary.

The Mary-Church image is, I suspect, the 'objective correlative' of the feeling-dimension, the restoration of which theology desperately needs. The notion of a totally free response on the part of humanity besides the response of Jesus to the Father was *felt* to be essential. The thought of Mary, far from problematizing a Christology of sinlessness, gives it larger breathing room. As well as the response destined to carry the world's whole burden of sin and thus to reveal its carrier as divine, there is the response that cannot carry this burden yet is unburdened by guilt. Sinlessness as communicable is highlighted by sinlessness that is not communicable. The humanity of God is highlighted by the perfection of humanity that is not God.

Finally, the ontological equality with God of him who not only has, but is able to give to others, emotional equality with God recalls the reasoning employed by the Council of Nicaea. With amazing intrepidity, that council saw that if Jesus does for us what only God can do, then he *is* God, whatever the appearances say of the enormity of a man, who wept and raged and died under torture, being by nature God. This intrepidity, said Lonergan, was a case of 'intellectual conversion': accepting an unavoidable judgement in spite of appearances, and thus opening new doors.

The concept of guiltlessness enables us to concentrate on the psychological newness, the startling strangeness, the dazzling otherness, of the world evoked for those who do not have it by him who has. In terms of this surprise at a 'brave new world' that was to collapse in ruins I have sought to understand the process of salvation. It fell to Jesus alone to be the agent of this surprise, of its disillusionment and of its eternal justification.

35. Apocalyptic and the New Life

The religious category in which the Resurrection of Jesus was placed was the resurrection which was to happen at the end of time. There would be an end to human history. 'The sea will give up its dead': the dead would all be raised to live for ever with God in a world unshadowed by death. Jesus, risen, was the beginning of this new world after history.

Why was this myth generated? What problem is it solving? What need is it fulfilling? Perhaps this myth is evidence that the human spirit, at the full stretch of its spiritual ambition, finds the fact of death unacceptable. In a world in which there is death, it is impossible to believe unequivocally and wholeheartedly in a God who invites us into his eternal friendship. Whatever our platonistic reasoning may say (and Americans are inveterate Platonists!), our feeling is thwarted by death from fully believing in such an eternal destiny. So what does the psyche do? It projects a beautiful new world after this one, where death shall have been swept away.

That world provided the category for Jesus' Resurrection. But the Christ-event, instead of fitting into and finally finding itself trapped within an ancient apocalyptic vision, goes to the root of that vision in the human psyche. It lays bare the fact that we find God's love incompatible with death because we see in death God's way of keeping us from his abundant life. The Christ-event deals with that unspeakable suspicion in the soul by having God die and thus forfeit all claim to this 'mastery'. The Resurrection of Jesus, as manifesting the life of the God who died out of love, has no need of a myth which precisely disguises the soul's suspicion of God by arranging for his final triumph, a deathless world.

Hence the Christian belief in Christ as the new life, as it matured in the writings of Paul, got freer and freer of its earlier apocalyptic matrix and became increasingly able to hold its own in this world, where death is fact. Jesus liberates us from the bondage of death by curing the soul's deep suspicion of God, not by diverting us from this suspicion into an apocalyptic dream.

The comparison of Jesus' sinlessness with Mary's reinforces a point of the utmost importance. In Mary we contemplate sinlessness purely as exemplar of our human condition in its liberated state, untrammelled by the primal guilt. We do not contemplate the source of our liberation. In her we see our human condition in its perfected state of friendship, or emotional equality, with God. We do not contemplate one who brings us into that friendship. We learn from this perfect exemplar, who is not the Saviour, that an exemplar as such is not saving.

The truth is itself salutary. The statement that an exemplar suffices, that it is enough to see and acknowledge our true condition in relation to God, is a mockery of our experience of alienation. Such experience goes too deep for this kind of 'saving' truth to dislodge it. Only God himself, by some direct communication, can tell us that in spite of our experience of guilt, of forlornness, of confinement to a self-contained human world, of being from time immemorial under the reign of death, we are his beloved and may live as his close friends.

The paradigmatic moment of this communication is the encounter with the risen Jesus. In that encounter, Jesus was seen as enjoying the eternal friendship of God, as having it for us. We knew in that moment that we have it from him, of him. 'Of his fulness we have all received.' We, with Mary, receive of that 'fulness'.

We have our human life so self-shaped, so separated from God, that neither God's inspiration alone nor the perfect human exemplar alone can bring us out into our true infinite climate of love, but only a human life with divine efficacy. Given this, the Spirit is given. Without this, the Spirit is confined to that prophetic inspiration which *hopes* for this. An exemplarist Christology, then, founders on the rock of our primal guilt. The uncomfortable thought occurs that perhaps a great deal of contemporary soteriology is not talking about salvation at all, only about encouragement.

Is this a depressing or pessimistic doctrine? Quite the reverse. It brings to us the glad tidings that what we call the normal is far more out of kilter than we imagined, and that therefore the condition which God would and will impart to us in Christ is further in advance of our present condition than we had thought. This stress on the gap between the 'normal' and the true was ever the message of the prophet, the mystic, the saint, the poet, the charismatic social critic. It doesn't make much sense to the bourgeois. Yet let us not be too hard on him, for we are saturated with his 'sensible' outlook and happy to be so. Again, the uncomfortable thought: Does not the western Church, as it emerges from Vatican II, represent an over-exuberance of the bourgeois mentality and a tendency to soteriologize accordingly?

36. Jesus' Own Story

The story line for the Great Story is constituted by the experience of the disciples of Jesus. The stages of the story are the stages of their development: the lyric stage, the desolation or death-of-God stage, and the new life. The stages, and the progressions, are provoked in them by Jesus as he (a) conjures up the Kingdom, (b) fails them and (c) comes to them bearing the new life. Not surprisingly, this recovery of the story line in its full vigour has found analogues throughout the world of Christian experience: the traditional Three Ages of the spiritual life, the tripartite structure of the Rosary, to say nothing of the great poetic developments in Eliot, Shakespeare and Dante, all of which show clearly the three phases of lyric, desolation, and new life.

Once the gospel story is established as the story of the original fellowship, the question of Jesus' own story becomes urgent. Where was he, how was it for him, as the story progressed for them through its stages and crises? This is not a question of curiosity. Rather, this question lies at the very heart of the story of Peter and the others, of the story for them. The man who raised for others the question of God's interest in human beings in its deepest existential form raised thereby the question of his own involvement in this drama of God and human beings. The question of how Jesus experienced and responded to this drama is the very question of Jesus' trustworthiness in the relationship between him and the disciples. A relationship which passed through these astonishing phases of make, break, and new make demands for its integrity the fullest possible presence and openness on the part of the initiator.

This is compatible with saying that Jesus' own mind may have been utterly beyond them at the time. The conclusion of the last paragraph means that Jesus must have had *that* personal involvement and openness to them which with their ever-deepening conversion in the Easter and Pentecostal period, would be discovered to have been his. Any close relationship which passes through the stages of distrust and alienation and climaxes in the conversion of one of the partners will provoke in the converted person the cry: 'What he must have been going through!'

To have the disciples of Jesus not going through this retrospect, to have them able to be indifferent or agnostic or still totally baffled as to the mind and heart of Jesus, is to void the relationship itself as the mediator of their conversion. Any idea of the life of Jesus as the mere catalyst or occasion of an experience in the disciples will take its place among the many versions of a reductionist or subjectivist Christology. Furthermore, if the mind of Jesus himself is something to which we can be indifferent, then he did not raise for his disciples the question of God's concern with human beings at the deepest existential level.

It was Jesus' freedom from guilt, and his privileged relationship with God, which led to the proposition, on the eve of Good Friday, that if Jesus failed God was no more. To posit this condition in Jesus is inevitably to raise the question of his own consciousness, involvement and decisiveness in the whole affair. The Story is the story of a relationship involving, as a relationship must do, the conscious participation of the initiating partner.

There is an important reason why the question of Jesus' conscious part has tended to slip from view in my ongoing inquiry. Once the death of God for the disciples has been envisaged, it becomes possible to understand the transforming event as the act of God. The love that transforms is not the attitude of Jesus to the disciples, regarded as *representing* the attitude of God, but is the loving presence of the infinite Mystery itself, its death a wonderful act of the lover's deference to man who prior to this revelation could not contemplate God without guilt. The enormous weight of explanation is thus taken off Jesus at this point, and this easily leads to the oversight that the conscious attitude of Jesus is not central to the whole affair. Nothing could be further from the truth. The new theological enablement to see the transformation as the work of God alone in all his infinity and mystery directs our gaze into the heart of Jesus as the place of God's working. If for Jesus to die was for God to die, who was Jesus alive, who was he for himself, what was his experience? The question of the psychology of Jesus bursts most powerfully from a totally God-centred soteriology.

119

We come to the question: Did Jesus experience the three stages? I shall confine myself to the first two, those of lyric and of desolation. The risen life of Jesus as experienced by him is, I think, beyond our comprehension. In any case what concerns us is his personal involvement in the crisis whose divine resolution is our salvation.

As to the first stage, the answer is clear. Since the whole enthusiasm and momentum of the movement stemmed from his experience of God's immediacy, he knew in the most acute form the ecstasy of those days. What he told them was coming he felt coming. According to Dunn's important work, *Jesus and the Spirit*,[3] he interpreted the power which worked in him for healing and exorcism in the light of his deep and inalienable sense of sonship. The principle of interpretation is crucial: the heart free of all guilt and bathed in the presence and loving power of God. It was no 'dogma' which convinced Jesus of his eschatological significance and role, as Schweitzer believed, but an immediacy to God whose total self-abasement justified the otherwise unjustifiable claim that, with his life, the Day of the Lord was dawning.

How did he envisage the violent end towards which he saw his mission as moving? More precisely, what in his experience corresponded to the feeling the disciples growingly had that if the movement failed God was no more? Is there any correspondence here? Or is there, on his side, only a sense of the fittingness of that death which would be for them unmitigated disaster? An affirmative here would negate the deepest movement in the drama as that movement occurs in their souls and, mysteriously, in his.

To understand that movement we have to return to one of the key principles of this book, the transcendental connection between a person's affair with God and the person's self-awareness. Self-awareness, I have insisted, is the trace or vestige of God. The consequent self-love is the initial turn-on in our love affair with God. Thus our love affair with God is the transformation of our self-awareness.

We naturally foresee death as the cessation of self-awareness. Thus the fact of death introduces an element of doubt and distrust into our relationship with God. While it is true that the fact of

[3] James D. G. Dunn, *Jesus and the Spirit: A Study of the Religious and Charismatic Experience of Jesus and the First Christians As Reflected in the New Testament* (Philadelphia: Westminster Press, 1975).

death has done at least as much to reinforce religion as to disable it, this reinforcement has not been felt in that part of religiousness where the personalness of God to the self-aware person is emphasized. This statement will be strongly contested and evidence adduced from much religious experience in which the acceptance of death has been the supreme act of personal trust in a personal Creator. But this is Christian experience. It depends on precisely that revolution in religious consciousness of which we are now examining the beginnings.

The personalness of God to the self-aware person is the cutting edge of religious consciousness. It clearly marks off Hebraic religiousness from its pagan neighbours. While the latter are content with monstrous and contradictory images of God, the Hebrew mentality holds God responsible, sometimes bitterly, for the passion for justice that burns in the human heart. If you want to see explored the equation of religiousness with human flourishing, you must go to the Bible. Now the people of the Bible, unlike their pagan neighbours, had very little in the way of a doctrine of the after-life. I leave it to scholars to say whether the later Jewish belief in immortality came largely from non-Jewish sources. I don't think it grew naturally out of the specifically Hebraic way of envisaging man's relationship with God. That vision was so passionately convinced of God's human life-promotingness that it perforce left in the shade (literally!) that side of the human experience where there is no life left to promote. 'The dead do not praise you, Lord', as the psalm says.

Thus the religiousness which is based on the personalness of God for the self-aware person is both the cutting-edge of religious consciousness *and* growingly in crisis with the fact of death. Let us not confuse the issue by calling this religiousness individualist. Quite to the contrary, it is when God and the flourishing of the heart's affections become indissolubly wedded in a culture that God becomes the God of a community, of a people.

What happens when the personalness of God for the self-aware person takes a quantum leap, as it does in the case of Jesus? Two completely opposed answers suggest themselves here. One answer is that such a person's consciousness reaches beyond death, no longer sees death as the obstacle or the snag in his religious self-awareness. Jesus would then be a sort of super-Socrates, his inner eye opened to that mystery which baffles humanity. The other and opposite answer is that for such a person the contrast between the presence of God and the fact of death would be more acute than for one who had not made the quantum leap into freedom from guilt. Of this I am now convinced.

The psychology of Jesus embraces, and unimaginably intensifies, all those movements of the human heart which have wedded God to life, to flourishing, to relationship, to community, to beauty seen and felt, to the smell of earth. Jesus is the magnificently spoilt child of God, the child who unequivocally believes in the spoiling and in his spoiler. There is absolutely nothing in Jesus of that sad pagan wisdom which only allows itself to half-enjoy. For Jesus death is even more 'the thing that doesn't fit' than it is for the Hebraic style of religiousness of which he is the full flowering.

Yet it loomed large for him. That fact is as important for the understanding of his psychology as is the fact of his weddedness to the God of life. Death loomed for Jesus not as the symbol of personal doubt of God, which it is for us, not as the question-mark on personal religiousness, which it is for us, not as the fatal weakness in the God-life equation, which it is for us, but as an incomprehensible obedience to that Power who gave him his mission and his meaning. For Jesus, death is lifted beyond all the ways in which we adjust it to our condition, into the sphere of pure obedience. It has no place in his life. It does not breathe its wisdom into his thought. It does not instil in him the message it instils in us: 'Ultimately you're on your own, you know, and without meaning'. It is starkly commanded, with an intention which he does not understand, which no one can understand, which only the faithful heart can know.

It is this lifting of death, for Jesus, out of being the agent of self-questioning which it is for us, into the sphere of an obedience, a mysterious destiny, that we have to think about when we consider his experience of the transition from the 'lyric' to the 'desolation'.

There is a strange development in the self-awareness of Jesus. In the lyric phase, the immediacy of God gives him the unmistakable sense of living, for everybody, what human life really is, a flourishing in the power and presence of God; a sense of his life as given to others as the first-fruits of the Reign of God. His life feels like it is for others. He personifies the Kingdom. Then, as the violent end looms, it too will be for others. The meaning of its inappropriateness for him is its being undergone for all. He came to know his

122

death as an act of love for humankind. It is the givenness by God for others which constitutes the unity of that amazing life, a unity spanning a God for whom there is no death, and death.

The personalness of God for self-awareness is the cutting-edge of religiousness because it is headed towards the resolution of guilt. Guilt is the brake on the orientation of self-love to the love of God, so the more we allow ourselves to be moved beyond self-love into the love of God, the closer we come to the dissolution of guilt. The continual pressure of guilt causes us to find in the fact of death, of the coming cessation of self-awareness, a welcome corroboration. Death 'proves' that myself-awareness and self-love are for me alone. So guilt welcomes death and, in so far as I am free of guilt, death is not welcome to me. If I am totally free of guilt, death is totally unwelcome. This is the psychology of Jesus, in which death is moved out of the sphere of welcome into the sphere of a mysterious obedience. In this position, death will function as the enablement for *God* to die and so dissolve guilt.

This is the psychology for Phil. 2:11 ff. The Pauline statement about one who, though the equal of God and pre-existent with God, chose to die, can also be seen in the shorter perspective of the psychology of Jesus. We see there one who is not partnered with death, who does not belong in the world of guilt-cankered self-love for which death is appropriate, embracing death only as an obedience to the infinite Mystery.

Now we can set the development in Jesus in the total picture of our salvation story. Death, for Jesus, is the opening of the door onto the death of God which the disciples will experience. It has no place in his life if that life is considered by itself. Death does not have for him the appropriateness it has for man in guilt, who must see in it a partner. Not being for him the seal of self-absorption, it is exclusively functional to the new state of affairs it will bring in for the disciples, namely the death of God.

Jesus does not welcome death. He accepts it at the hands of God. Centuries of Christian experience have blurred this enormous difference. A profoundly correct instinct led Paul to see the death of Jesus as an obedience, not as the natural consummation which Christian humanism pictures, nor as the crowning moment of the martyr or the hero. It is as an obedience that the death of Jesus is the instrument of God's saving design and reflects that design. It is as an obedience that it finds its metaphor in the sacrificial lamb rather than in the martyr. The death of Jesus is the mysterious end to the magic world of spiritual childhood which centres upon a heart without guilt. It is that negation which only God as love can undo, and even this love can only effect the undoing by undoing itself in death.

We seem to have been subjectively verifying the old Pauline axiom that death is the wages of sin. We appropriate this axiom when we understand how our guilt-induced disbelief in our self as God-inclined finds its corroboration in the knowledge that one day the self will be no more. 'The wages of sin' becomes 'the reward of guilt, the appropriate partner for guilt'. So strong is death in this partnership that only the death of God, which is the love of God in its tenderest manifestation, can break it.

The Pauline concept of death as 'the wages of sin' is a pointer to that most radical view of death which alone can mediate an understanding of God's transforming action at the point of the story where death is centre-stage. A big mistake has occurred over this Pauline concept, which has been taken to mean only that death is caused by sin, that if it weren't for sin there wouldn't be death. As this idea overstrains belief, the Pauline concept is quietly dropped. It is only when we begin to appropriate these ancient ideas that we start looking for another meaning in Paul's statement. We see that it can shed light on the deepest and darkest things in our psychology.

The appropriateness of death for guilt is, we learn from Paul, the thing to explore. It is a subjective appropriateness: that is what 'appropriation' is about. It is a deep sense, engendered by guilt, of death as right for us. This feeling is an enfeeblement of our belief in ourselves having any ultimate significance. It finds in the fact of death by far its most potent endorsement. Voegelin is right to say that insofar as the human spirit in history follows the clues offered by the infinite Mystery, it pursues immortality: which does not mean an escape from, or a disregard or forgetfulness of, death, but a refusal to use death as the corroboration of an unambitious spirituality. This refusal is the loosening of our guilt-entrapment, the rallying of the enfeebled spirit in the presence of the Spirit, the taking of a most precious hint from a distant country.

Jesus, the guiltless one, took that hint wholly and let his life assemble round that self-valuation which the hint enjoins. He valued himself as the intimate of the infinite Mystery, and so threw off the death in which our enfeebled spirits find the confirmation of their feebleness. Death, to his feeling, did not have that appropriateness it has for us. The cross casts a heavy shadow over the Galilean mission that is really a shadow, really an alien, really an evil presence. It is only in a light brighter than was available in the time of the mission that the shadow will disappear. That light is the Resurrection. If the mission was shadowed for them it was shadowed for him too. He experienced, in the most acute form, the alienness of death to what was going on in him and around him. Death was for him what death truly is: an enigma to which God alone, a mysterious love alone, holds the key. It was not what it is for human culture: the partner, the portentous endorsement of spiritual triviality.

What happens when we fail to take the hint from Paul, when we fail to realize that the worst thing we do with death is not to flee it or forget it, but to enthrone it and make ourselves its subjects? We then go up to a shallower level of our being where a different story is appropriate. At that level, my self-esteem sends me in search of an independent significance for myself, initiates the ego-project, does not understand itself as the opening of a love affair with the Infinite, but on the contrary tries to be God. At that level death is the alien, the enemy of my godhead. At that level death has to be befriended if I am to grow spiritually. It is fatal to confuse this befriending of death with that befriending which at the deeper level is a spiritual temptation. Death tries to tell me that I am not God, and that is a good word. Death also tries to tell me that I have no ultimate value, and that is the worst of words. Not to discern the difference between the good word and the bad word is the most serious failure in discernment, the confusion of humility with spiritual unambitiousness.

Thus Becker is making a true diagnosis when he finds everywhere the denial of death, but it becomes a false diagnosis when it claims to be ultimate. The radical spiritual sickness of man is not his flight from death but his acceptance of death as the last word. It is this that puts him in flight from death. It is the flight from a taskmaster who should not be master at all. Becker has highlighted what man does to make do with a situation in which death quenches our spiritual zest, but it is the situation, not our attempts to escape it, which is the evil. It is to the situation that God points when he puts his man among us, surrounds his life with miracle and shows human life as a stranger to death, thus setting it on the course towards the ultimate crisis of humanity which only God's death in love will resolve.

Our sickness is a spiritual torpor which prevents our life from being God's self-showing because it is shadowed by death. God's remedy is to dramatize for us our life as his to the extent of outlawing death, of making alien our oldest partner; and then, with the scene properly set, with the record set straight as to who man truly is, bringing us beyond the Kingdom of Death into his Kingdom. The Kingdom of Death is where death is the measure of the human spirit. The confrontation of Jesus with death, as exemplified in the strong, affirmative, healing note of the Galilean mission, is the denial of that measure. This is the meaning of the traditional imagery in which Jesus is seen as battling with death and overcoming. This meaning, like the Pauline 'wages of sin', cannot come through until we clear the deepest level of self-appropriation, where not the denial of death but the befriending of it is the temptation of the Evil One, who hates the God in man.

What a labour it is to clarify that one death which is an act of love for God and for all that he has made, for God and his beautiful world! It is the labour of clearing this death from the approximations of our partial vision of the good: the tragic hero, the martyr to a cause. All these images are shaped within the Kingdom of Death. They image people who have done nobler things with our situation than most of us do. They do not provide the measure for him who breaks that situation. They get their meaning from him, not he from them.

PART IV—RETRACTATIONS

37. Retractation 1

In my last book, *The Crucified Is No Stranger,* I did not grasp the radical orientation of the self to God. I saw the self as oriented towards freedom from what I then called generic guilt. This I now see as merely infant-guilt, that pressure of the 'psychic womb' in all its forms, including the superego, which rebukes the individual initiative. I have since come to see generic guilt or original sin (the equivalence is now clear) as the deep sense of 'failing the other' and, ultimately, of failing that mysterious other who is God. The human being is freed from this real, 'adult', generic guilt only by that radical transformation in which the God whom guilt can see only as power is seen in truth to be love. This is another way of describing how the human being, congenitally in love with God but unable through guilt to believe in God's love for him, is enabled for this belief. This is the true freeing of the human being, that conferred by the Yes of the Beloved. Of this enablement by the infinite to love the infinite, of this liberation from the terrible guilt-inducing pressure of the infinite, the freeing I portrayed in my last book is a pale, romantic shadow. It is of the self in freedom from guilt to love the infinite, and not of the self conceived outside this relationship that Jesus is the exemplar.

The next question is: How does this exemplar bring out what I now see to be the real self, the lost lover of the infinite that holds it trapped in guilt? Does the exemplar 'evoke' this deep self? If so, the *memory* of a historical Jesus now assimilated to the true Christ-self would suffice. But the liberation, by the Christ-self-exemplar, of the Christ-self in the human being, can only be a direct self-manifestation of God, of God as love and not as power. Yet the Christ-self-exemplar is the agent of this divine liberating action: that is the whole idea of an exemplar Christology. He is, then, at once human-exemplar and divine. But it is impossible for the Christ-self-exemplar to have this divine nature through some sort of vision or intuition on the part of the human being to be liberated. What an extraordinary process in the one being liberated: to elevate the Jesus of history to the divine level, and so to experience liberation at his hands! That makes us the saviour of Jesus, not Jesus of us. If the Christ-self-exemplar as represented by Jesus is to be divine as well as human, it is Jesus himself whose divinity must be declared by God to the soul. That declaration by God must have been 'heard' at the very start of the Christian preaching.

The Christ fallacy consists in seeing the divinity of Jesus in the human universality of the Christ archetype. It has always intrigued me that in Christology, especially in its liturgical and devotional aspect, the assertion of the divinity of Jesus has always been via some universal human figure: Messiah-King and Son of Man in the early Jewish days of Christianity, *Kurios, Dominus, Rex* in the succeeding gentile age. Some form of representative humanity, some 'ideal type', has always been found indispensable to the full constitution of Jesus Christ in the believing mind. For our more self-aware and introspective culture, 'the self' as understood for instance by Jung, that obscure centre in each of us which is not the ego and calls the ego to ever-wider consciousness, seems the appropriate successor to those ideal-types in which an earlier, more extroverted age concentrated its sense of a fuller human existence.

It is easy to confuse this human universality of Jesus with his divinity, while it is in fact the cultural mediation of his divinity. It is that human sense of 'the one man', the Son of Man, the *Anthropos,* which the psyche produces in response to the Palestinian who brought his followers along a new way that climaxed in the revelation of the Father in the Son through the Spirit. It is only the mediation of the Palestinian's new and eternal status. So at the very beginning he was called 'the Christ' but was known as a Christ who carried in himself the whole mystery of God and so was an agent of God's deep design, which infinitely exceeds our culture-crystallized conception of the new age, of the Kingdom. In the same way today, the universal self which he properly evokes is a self whose meaning and destiny are, literally, infinitely beyond all possible human conceptions of man's place in the universe.

What Christians believe to have been the decisive moment in history, God's self-disclosure in Jesus Christ, has raised problems ever since. It could not be otherwise, for the attempt faithfully to appropriate that moment brings into play all a person's cultural resources and freshly surprises his or her way of seeing the world by introducing into that vision a new, deeper, and always disturbing center. Each new culture is thus a fresh theatre for this surprise and will put different questions to the faith of the Incarnation.[1] How complicated and untidy that process is can be seen, for instance, in Lonergan's book *The Way to Nicea,* in which is described how the first great cultural appropriation slowly found the enablement to become clear and explicit.

The problem faced by Nicaea was: How could a human being be said in truth to be God without involving us in a string of contradictions? It would be false to say that the Council solved this problem by mere logical ingenuity. The solutions arrived at involved a real stretching of the mind beyond its normal limits. Lonergan is able to show in what that mind-stretch consisted. Most of us most of the time wobble in practice between 'naive realism' ('A thing is what it looks and feels like') and 'critical realism' ('A thing is known by what it does'). The statement of Nicaea, that the son is 'of the same substance' as the Father, will, if by 'substance' we understand 'stuff' (naive realism), mean either that the Son and the Father are merely two 'sides' of the same 'bit of stuff', or that the 'bit of stuff' is split in two. In the first case you have 'two aspects of God', in the second 'two Gods', both of which are heretical. Thus the Nicene statement is only coherent if we understand it as critical realists. Then we have to say, with Athanasius, that the Son is all that the Father is and does, all that the Father does (the realist criteria), except being Father and generating. In this understanding, the mind is rigorously denied its 'piece of stuff', even the spiritualized piece of stuff which interposes itself into all minds who try to handle spiritual realities. There truly is such a thing as 'reason illumined by faith', which gives us a real sense of God as a reality in his own right and not relative to human concerns: a sort of rational equivalent of 'We give thee thanks for thy great glory' or, as C. S. Lewis puts it, 'Thank you for being you'—a prayer stance of which we have never stood in greater need.

Nevertheless, the question faced by Nicaea is limited to the 'how' of the divinity of Jesus, a question which cannot be answered without arriving at a concept of the Trinity. There is a new question today: How is Jesus known to be God? By faith, assuredly. But

[1] Cf. H. Richard Niebuhr, *Christ and Culture* (New York: Harper and Row).

this answer does not really tackle the question, any more than it would have met the requirements of Nicaea. As at Nicaea, so now, the question about Jesus challenges the mind of the questioner. As then, so now, it calls on the mind's best resources. Whereas at the time of Nicaea those resources were centred in inquiry into the nature of the real, today they are centred in the exploration of human experience. There are many signs that this exploration is reaching a point where we ask: 'How does human experience, in all its psychic depth, reflect objective reality?' This is what is involved in the evolution of the question 'Who am I?' via the question 'Who am I to you?' to the question 'Why am I?' In other words, a new God-consciousness, a new trembling of consciousness in the presence of its constituting mystery, may be trying to be born. This may be the reason why the christological question, always an accurate barometer of changing culture, is beginning to be : 'What conceivably could be that experience of God which would have to express itself in the words "Jesus is God"?'

The subject is Jesus, a person who has been with us for two millennia, not just the Christ-archetype. So this experience, whatever it may be, must have been enjoyed since the beginning of the Christian preaching. Moreover, an experience new to humankind is best studied in its beginning when experience was all that the people concerned had to go on, when there was no room, or not so much room, for the human proclivity to think one is reporting experience when in reality one is merely importing an idea from memory. F. R. Leavis at Cambridge read an indifferent sonnet by Emily Brontë and commented: 'She thinks she feels like that but she doesn't feel like that.' Furthermore, the first documentation of Jesus Christ lays a heavy overt stress on experience: the manifestations of the Spirit, the new peace and joy, the dispelling of fear. As one would rather expect! Everything seems to point towards the experience of the disciples of Jesus as the locus for our new christological question.

One may reply: 'We can know virtually nothing about the experience of those remote figures, about whose very names scholars are in dispute. This will be a work of pure conjecture, without any control.' The following considerations may be helpful.

First, the question is real and urgent. It will not be silenced. It pertains to that psychological and cultural mediation of faith which, suppressed, makes the statements of faith sound hollow and perfunctory. Second, the type of experience in question pertains to those deeper levels which always surprise us by their universality compared with our day-to-day concerns. The way an anonymous English mystic in the fourteenth century describes contemplative prayer is a most succinct and exact description of what I try in my fumbling way to do when I pray. The author of *The Cloud of Unknowing* writes: 'Therefore I will leave on one side everything I can think, and choose for my love that thing which I cannot think.' Centuries later, Abbot Chapman wrote: 'Hence in "contemplation" the intellect faces a blank and the will follows it.'[2] Third, we are beginning to learn to universalize human experience in a new way. The first two parts of this book are an attempt to do just this. There I am attempting to fashion the tools with which, in the third part, I address myself to the consciousness of Jesus and his interaction with his followers.

Above all, the decision to remain agnostic about the experience of the disciples has to face the question: 'What do I believe about Jesus?' If I am prepared to envisage a man walking this earth the intimate of God and a stranger to sin, how can I withhold the admission that he must have had a devastating effect on the people who came close to him and whom he admitted into this intimacy? It might be objected: 'To believe that Jesus was sinless is part of the Christian faith-stance. You can't use it to write history.' I agree, although I would reject the assumption often underlying this objection, that something held by faith cannot make good sense of a historical event. This is one of those sacred dichotomies which have ravaged our understanding.

My main purpose in writing this book is to speak from faith to faith. The Christian faith can generate within itself a certain visionary quality desperately needed, which would transfigure our ordinary experience. For this, a meeting-point must be found between Christian faith and contemporary self-understanding. For me, that meeting-point has been the sinlessness of Jesus which, in relation to man's ultimate purpose, raises the question 'Why? Why a sinless man?' and, in relation to our human world and its cultures, raises the question 'Who? Who could this be?' The reason for the Christian tradition's insistence on the sinlessness of Jesus is a conviction that the mystery of our faith begins with the ministry of

---

[2] *The Spiritual Letters of Dom John Chapman* (Sheed and Ward), p. 76.

133

Jesus. I have tried to bring out the deepest implication of this conviction: that the ministry of Jesus prepares for the death of God and for a consequent revelation which might, on my presuppositions, be understood more deeply than heretofore to be revelation.

There is also a broader assumption behind this enterprise: a fundamental belief in a community of human experience across the great stretches of human time and human space. It is the sort of belief Eliot had. Eliot 'knew' what Shakespeare was trying to do, knew it very accurately by his own attempts to create poetry. He even saw a 'successful poem' as calling some poet of the past into dialogue. He saw poets carrying on a conversation about human experience across the reaches of time. It is part of the greatness of Shakespeare that Hamlet invited the inquiries of Freud who, by his interest, showed the abiding contemporaneity of Shakespeare. It is the mark of a great human work of self-expression to admit into its intimacy the quite other concerns of a much later age. How pre-eminently true this is of 'the moment in and out of time'. The centre of that moment is the consciousness of Jesus, but it is above all the communication of this consciousness to which we must attend. For that involved a drama of blood in which the receivers of the communication knew, individually and as a community, dissolution and received, into a new emptiness of the spirit, the Word made flesh.

38. Retractation 2

The concept of 'the self' as distinct from the ego, the concept of an identity incomparably wider and deeper than the one I live with, is indispensable for a modern Christology. The union of the person with Christ cannot be adequately conceived of if we ignore those hints that come, through dreams, through images which come between sleep and waking and through those significant interruptions of experience which Eliot evokes so well, of an altogether larger self.

> For most of us, there is only the unattended
> Moment, the moment in and out of time,
> The distraction fit, lost in a shaft of sunlight,
> The wild thyme unseen, or the winter lightning
> Or the waterfall, or music heard so deeply
> That it is not heard at all, but you are the music
> While the music lasts. These are only hints and guesses,
> Hints followed by guesses; and the rest
> Is prayer, observance, discipline, thought and action.
> The hint half guessed, the gift half understood, is Incarnation.

Just as 'the Christ' and 'the Son of Man' were once the psychic bait whereby the new believer was caught by the new life and set on the new way, so the wider self we can experience today must be the bait whereby the life catches us.

But it is only the bait, and 'bait' is only a metaphor. Another metaphor is that 'the self' is the 'place' in the psyche where the new life is 'inserted'. A less metaphorical statement would be that 'the self' is what is becoming newly aware and central for a person who believes in Christ. Such a person is surprising himself, is amazed at the new energies which seem to be released within him. He recognizes those energies as his own, as a wider life of *himself* of which he had been unaware.

There are times, in prayer, when I have to say that this larger current of my life is flowing with an energy not its own, that it has a direction altogether beyond the direction sometimes taken by a flow of images: a direction as certainly all-transcending as the energy is certainly from some mysterious source not myself. This Godward-tending self which is, transiently, the life of my self and which takes me much further than 'I' could go, is a reality I recognize in a certain story, and in no other way: the story of Jesus, of his journey to 'the Father' which is for us the progressive revelation of the Father in him. In *Jesus and the Spirit,* the only spiritually oriented book of exegesis I know, James D. G. Dunn says that Jesus showed his followers who they really were, awoke them to a new identity they could only have from him. I have to say: 'That is exactly right. That is my experience.'

It seems that the cost of being directed towards infinity as personal, of being directed infinitely beyond the reach even of my 'deep self', is the surrender to a human being whom the infinite shows to be of its own nature. Perhaps the human psyche, vast city and even greater jungle and desert of the soul, stands between the infinite and the physical, between the mystery and history. For the psyche to be reborn it must be energized by God's union between the historical and himself, God's union passing through the psyche as Spirit. When John talks of being reborn 'of the Spirit', does he mean the ineffable mystery joined to a historical man, the juncture being the Holy Spirit, *in* the reborn? Is it in the Spirit that we understand that Jesus coming 'in water and blood' is the new life; that the ineffable beginning, the *arche,* is the source of the new life; and that the energy not our own with which we move to the infinite has its direction *from* the former *to* the latter?

I am intrigued with the idea that in saying that the Father and the Son are 'of the same nature', you make of the nature a kind of impersonal backcloth to both of them, which will never do. Naive realism? Has that 'spiritual bit of stuff' got back in? Perhaps what really keeps that 'spiritual bit of stuff' out is the belief, so vibrant in the very beginning, that the oneness of the Father and the Son is itself personal, identity, mystery, Holy Spirit. The outpouring of the Spirit, the falling-upon of the Spirit, was so central to the first experience, that the Spirit was thought of as the nerve of the otherwise inconceivable oneness of the Leader with the ineffable mystery they had worshipped in temple and synagogue.

In sum, while 'the self', personification of the far-reaching psyche, is that in us which comes alive when we 'put on Christ', it comes alive with a life not its own. It moves out to a destiny infinitely beyond the reach of human conceiving, though not beyond the reach of human desire. It thus knows a freedom infinitely beyond human conceiving. The welcoming beyondness is represented at once by the ineffable mystery in which all life moves and by what Wallace Stevens calls 'that old catastrophe'. When, mysteriously, we know that these are one, it is the Spirit who is moving in us. I am now convinced that the difference between accepting the Incarnation as traditionally believed and not accepting it is the difference between really believing in an infinite destiny for humankind and not so believing.

If it is only 'in the Spirit' that we can know and savor Jesus, and not just the Christ-archetype, as that in us which moves inerrantly towards the infinite, an important consequence follows. The divine status and function of the historical man Jesus, the eternal divinity of that Palestinian, is not something which can be thought of by itself. It can only be thought of in so far as we are possessed by the Spirit who binds Jesus and the Father. We are not confronted with the oneness of Jesus with the Father. That oneness moves in us as a life whereby we know, feel, are inward to that oneness. The Holy Spirit is not an added mystery. He is the gracious availability to us of the one mystery. He translates the Incarnation from impossibility into life, our life. Perhaps the difficulty of believing the Incarnation has been that, with the role of the Spirit virtually forgotten, we are denying ourselves the infinite aid to the understanding of this belief, and so confronting the Incarnation as an infinite problem. An infinite problem is a contradiction in terms. To leave out the Holy Spirit is to deny ourselves that inwardness to the Father-Jesus oneness which came, as part of the 'new deal', when Jesus was encountered after his death.

A friend stated the problem exactly: 'Isn't it strange that distorted forms of Christianity always get the Holy Spirit wrong, while the Holy Spirit is precisely our infallible aid for getting the whole thing right?' I came to get the Holy Spirit 'right', or at least to feel much more comfortable theologically in this area, through 'breaking-out' the original impact of the Easter encounter as a psychological displacement of divinity from 'God' to Jesus: there followed naturally, as it were refining on this, an extension of divinity from 'God' to Jesus, which became, equally naturally, the personal life of this extension. This means that the Holy Spirit is closely wedded to the stretching of the psyche under the impact of the Easter encounter. In other words, the Holy Spirit encourages us to experience the newly exploded divine status of Jesus, and enables us to do so. It is Jesus of Nazareth, not just the Christ-archetype, who moves in us; but that it is he, is to be felt in the Spirit. The Spirit is an infinite balancing of the infinite imbalance of 'Jesus of Nazareth' and 'the infinite'. So much theology of the Incarnation has been the attempt to make sense of the infinite imbalance by itself, to unite conceptually the infinite and the man Jesus, whereas this takes infinite wisdom, which is the Spirit's gift to us. This attempt provokes its denial, as in *The Myth of God Incarnate,* which is the negation of a distortion.

The statement 'No one can say "Jesus is Lord" except in the Holy Spirit' is not only saying 'Without the Spirit you can't', but 'With the Spirit you can, though without the Spirit you will think you can't'. It is an encouraging, not an off-putting statement, but we pick up negative meanings so much more easily.

It is so easy to be moved by the story of Jesus up to the death and burial, to see in this the universal human story of hope and trust, with its inevitably enigmatic conclusion, and then to say that this story is so profound and all-embracing that a kind of universal self in all people has picked it up and transfigured it, and that thus we pass from the Jesus of history to the Christ of faith. To the contrary, the meaning of the Holy Spirit is that the transfiguring of Jesus into the universal Christ is not the work of the human psyche, so fertile in transformations and yet so incapable of generating saving truth, but of God. In this work, the transformative power of the psyche is not denied. It shines forth from the majestic figure in the Byzantine apse, in the haunting Christ of Cefalu. But the psyche's power is instrumental, mediatory. The transfiguring is of the Holy Spirit, and it is a transfiguring, not a transforming.

As against the psyche's inexhaustible power to translate everything into life and to make of death itself a transformation, the Spirit awakes in the believer the memory of that death and reminds him that there God died so that he could appear in the risen Jesus as the God of love. If God has had to die, we should hesitate

138

before we speak of death as transformation. In that hesitation, the eternal appears and welcomes us, for that hesitation is the Good Friday interim. Our affair with death is more serious than we think. Deeper than all the transformation myths we generate around death, our affair with death has in it an envious distrust of the eternal. The death of God is speaking to that distrust; and the life of God in the risen Jesus embraces a people for whom that distrust has at last fallen away. For that people, the death of Jesus is the theme of unending gratitude. For that people, Jesus alive is God alive. The life which they are given to know as alone life can be known, as their own, is the Holy Spirit.

We are in a world of meanings beyond the purview of the psyche. It is precisely the world of spirit, of movement in response to the infinite Spirit. To our belonging to that world, the Jesus who awoke men's hearts to the eternal and then exposed them to the death of the eternal is indispensable. He cannot disappear into the Christ, because his life and death have changed forever the meaning of that name. It is significant that Bultmann, who more than any other theologian has detached the Christ of the Kerygma from the Jesus of history, admitted that he had never understood the Holy Spirit!

39. Retractation 3

Soteriology is the attempt to answer the old question: How is the crucifixion of Jesus salvific? In my last book I tried to answer the question in the following way. The true self desires communion with God, but we recoil from this, our essential direction. This 're-coil' is the worst thing about us. We have to experience and acknowledge it at its worst if we are to be saved—the necessary condition. The sufficient condition is knowing that God accepts us even at this our worst. We see our 'recoil' at its worst in the killing of Jesus, for Jesus represents and lives out in its single-hearted fullness our true self. The motivation of the killing of Jesus is the desire to annihilate, to remove from our troubled lives, that desire for communion with God which is in us and would demand some unbearable exercise of our freedom.

In this theory the correct name for the evil disposition is fear rather than guilt: the fear of following our desire for God. It is true that I defined guilt as an unhappiness with freedom: 'feeling bad about feeling free'. But our unhappiness with freedom only merits the name of guilt when the guilt is that induced in someone by the 'psychic womb', whether family or institution or peer group, when he tries to be his own person. In other words it is 'infant guilt'. But true guilt, adult guilt, the feeling of failing another person or, at the limit, failing the mysterious otherness in which we 'live and move and have our being', is not the same thing as unhappiness with freedom. The latter condition is much more appropriately named fear.

While the power and influence of fear and dread in human life can hardly be overestimated, all I am concerned to say in this chapter is that it is not our root evil. If my earlier theory made fear the root evil, it cannot stand. Certainly the Christian story is of the dissolving of fear, but more radically it is the dissolving of guilt: of that 'adult guilt' which, we have seen, equates with original sin.

The real difficulty appears, however, when we ask how the negative tendency in the human is acted out in the crucifixion, for here a decision has to be made. Is it necessary to have the story of human evil and its divine dissolution lived through by its first participants who, in the end, speak and write to us out of their own experience of salvation; or does it suffice that the story exists now, for us to identify with the various participants as the Ignatian method and other meditation techniques taught us to do? I am in no doubt now that we have to take the first option. To settle for the second is to say 'It's the story that matters', in a way which implicitly denies the necessity of the *event* of salvation. There is a danger that the contemporary fascination, in theological circles, with 'stories' will obscure the event-requirement in the great story. The average student in my theology class can see the difference between salvation by a story and salvation by a person, but this difference is not always so clear to scholars.

In my last book, I did not face the above decision. It had not yet presented itself, though I think I felt myself fending it off. The result was that the crucifixion story slipped into a kind of middle ground. It did involve a real, sinless Jesus. It obviously involved real crucifiers, but they were merely representative of the human evil. They were not, to use a medical analogy, the patient who at the end of the story would be cured. Thus they were not in the drama of sin and its redemption the way Jesus was. He was in it as the Redeemer. They were not in it as the redeemed. So the story was not a story of salvation, meaning a story of definite people being saved or at least experiencing salvation.

While the Saviour was in the original event, there were no saved, but only crucifiers representing the awful way all of us who constantly need salvation behave. Without the saved there creeps in that fatal ambiguity which, in face of the legitimate question 'How did Jesus save us?', answers: 'That's up to you. Just let the story work on you.'

There is no way of telling the story as the story of salvation using the crucifiers, the people who wanted Jesus out of the way, as the protagonists for 'the sinner' in that story of sinners' salvation. I missed a hint from the story itself, since its main protagonist says: 'They do not know what they are doing.'

The sinner-protagonist must enter the story as sinner and exit from it as saved. That is to say, his sin must be somehow made overt by the event and, thus overt, be cured in the event. The sin that is made overt by the event must be sin as most radically and universally conceived. It must be the negative relationship to the ultimate mystery as that relationship is understood after a carefully built-up theory of the human condition in relation to that mystery.

The only possible sinner-protagonist is the disciples of Jesus, for they are the only saved participants in the story. I began to be aware of this once I came to see the resurrection encounter as salvific, as sin-dissolving. This made the disciples the saved ones, the pardoned ones, so they had to be in some sense 'the villain of the piece'.

In his massive recent book Schillebeeckx[3] seems to define the disciples' sin as their desertion of Jesus and the resurrection encounter as their reconciliation and forgiveness. This is inadequate, because the desertion of Jesus illustrates the universal human evil conceived of as fear, not as guilt. As deserters, the disciples line up with the people who want Jesus out of the way. Like them, they want 'out' from this frightening thing Jesus seems to stand for. The motive is fear, or dread, not guilt, although the desertion produces guilt. Such a motive does not show man's negative attitude to God at its most radical: fear or dread does not show man at issue with God in the direct way that guilt does. Fear's immediate object is not God but 'what may be involved in following my God-direction', whereas guilt has to do directly with being a creature, for it is a disaffection with creaturehood. It is not possible to find this truly universal sin in the desertion of Jesus.

Further, if the story is being adequately interpreted, whatever role the resurrection is said to have must be a role that resurrection alone could play. Do we need a resurrection from the dead to bring peace to the hearts of those who have failed the living? An apparition or a good dream is able to do as much. To say that the resurrection has as its main function one performed by an apparition or a dream is to say that the resurrection encounter is in the same order as the apparition and the dream. Since it is becoming increasingly clear that belief or disbelief in the resurrection consists primarily in how one regards the encounter with the risen Jesus, it

---

[3] Edward Schillebeeckx, *Jesus: An Experiment in Christology* (New York: The Seabury Press, 1979), p. 19.

is vital not so to interpret the whole story as to leave that encounter in the twilight zone of the psyche.

It is perhaps significant that at least one sympathetic critic of Schillebeeckx's book singled out for adverse comment only the treatment of the resurrection. I am sure Schillebeeckx believes in the resurrection, but does his current theology? And did mine when I held a similar view? I made much use of John Knowles' *A Separate Peace*.[4] I suggested that if, when Gene was paying his visit to 'the tree'—scene of the accident to his friend for which he had been responsible—on that dank November afternoon, Finny had suddenly bounded onto the scene alive and well and had embraced him, that would have been the sort of thing the resurrection encounter was. This is tantamount to the admission that the dream is the appropriate place for the return of the forgiving dead. Since the reconciling-the-deserter action was central to my account I was classing the resurrection encounter with the dream. In any case, the whole idea is much too small, individualist and romantic. The admission has to be made that, while I have always assented with the Church to the statement that Jesus is God, his being God played no necessary part, until recently, in my soteriological speculations.

We come at last to the big question: How does the universal sin, the original guilt, appear in the disciples of Jesus in the Great Story? What does it mean for the universal, original sin or guilt to 'appear'? This cannot refer to something done or not done by the disciples. One can't commit original sin. Nothing one does can be original sin itself made manifest. This is another reason why the crucifying of Jesus, or the handing him over, or the wanting him out of the way, cannot be *the* sin in the story. What we mean by the original sin 'appearing' is a universal state of soul coming to a head, coming to its crisis. This it does when the disciples' positive relationship to God has been brought, under the influence of Jesus, to a uniquely advanced state of development, so that their ultimate entrapment in this world, where guilt enthrones death as ruler and casts death's shadow on God, is highlighted.

Most wretched men they are: led on to the heights by their God-filled leader, they stand at last naked, rubbing their eyes as the immemorial jailer wakes them from their apocalyptic dream. Origi-

[4] *A Separate Peace* (New York: Macmillan).

nal sin, as it then appears in them, is the human captivity in the pure state, as it appears, and can only appear, when the great world of God has shown itself, as it uniquely did to the followers of Jesus, and is now rendered unreal.

Sin is the unreality of God. Never was the unreality of God such a poignant experience as it was for those people who had 'seen' him but now, in the face of the normal human world as it resumes its inexorable course and prepares to stamp out the one who had exposed God to them, must say that what they saw was nothing. Never did the fact of our mortality and the mortality of all our projects operate so efficaciously as the pretext for that deep distrust of our life which casts the shadow of guilt onto God. Never was man so totally captive in this world, its reality the only reality.

This condition, what Paul calls 'the flesh', is, outside the Good Friday interval, never realized in the pure state. Always the prisoner admits some rays of the transcendent to fall on the floor of his cell and delight his fitful gaze. At this turning- point of history, this inconclusive affair with the infinite breaks down. A small bunch of not too distinguished men and women are called upon to show to the people of all future time human autonomy, the human world as the only world, in all its bleakness.

The most important thing about the Good Friday condition is this: Not only is sin or guilt present in the pure state, but sin or guilt is wholly translated into desolation, wholly realized as desolation. The sense of failing another has got swallowed up in a sense of total isolation, that aching emptiness of the person that is always the source of guilt. Normally the sense of guilt feeds on our relatedness to God and to others, but in its pure state it swallows up everything in itself. It becomes the inner emptiness which has empowered it to spoil our relationships.

This ultimate condition of guilt as isolation and desolation is beyond self-accusation. If it does come to feel again the healing touch of the other, it will know better than to respond with self-accusation. Sometimes in a relationship-breakdown, a person is so deeply broken that he learns something of himself that is beyond self-accusation. With this he will be able to respond to a fresh initiative from the other in an absolutely simple and humble way, without the self-accusation that is always in part a cover. How inexorably one finds one's most 'frontier' experiences embedded in the great story!

144

The capital point is that if guilt is wholly translated into desolation, the lifting of desolation will be the lifting of guilt. We are at the heart of the principle that guilt is dissolved by love alone. The meaning of that principle is that the love of another can dissolve my guilt by getting behind it, as it were, to my emptiness, whence I create the destructive dimension of my relationships.

The ultimate desolation, whose lifting will be the lifting of the ultimate guilt, is the death of God. Metaphorically we could say that the shadow cast upon God by guilt has become total blackness in which God is no more. Anything that lifts this desolation which is the absence of God can only be the touch of God. It would be known by experience as the touch of God. Now we know by doctrine that guilt is lifted by God alone. The Good Friday condition translates this doctrinally known truth into its experiential equivalent: a desolation that is lifted by God alone, who is thus known to be God *by* the lifting of the desolation. Thus in the lifting of this desolation, the knowledge that guilt is no more is indivisibly the knowledge that God is here. In other words, God himself is experienced as taking away the guilt which was never till then wholly absent from our relationship with him. God himself? Jesus. Spirit. All is given in this moment: the lifting of guilt, the divinity of Jesus, the inundation of the Holy Spirit, the eternal friendship. At this molten moment, everything that will subsequently be doctrine is experience.

Once the death of God has 'worked' in this way, acted as pivot between the old worship and the new, it is seen as the working of God's love. At this crucial moment, the assertion of our-world-alone is not countered by God with the claim of his world, which would reawaken guilt, but is allowed to stand. In that new silence at the heart of man there is the possibility of knowing the touch of God without guilt, of knowing the voice of God without fear, of coming into the eternal friendship which cannot know guilt, and of knowing God as God when he comes.

Thus the death of God in the crucifixion of Jesus is not, in its deepest and controlling sense, the exposure of God in the person of Jesus to the injustice of this world, to act as the abiding critique of this world's values. It is that, but not in its essence; that is not its 'why'. If that is taken to be the essence, the death of God merely perpetuates, at a new level, the guilt of which it is properly the dissolution. That would be the very last word in the guilt-game, God

145

saying: 'You killed *me!*' Why do we always move straight from the 'Blessed Passion' to critique and not to sorrow, healing and joy, the delicious embarrassment of the forgiven which has no guilt in it? In so far as we do this we are insufficiently attentive to the Spirit.

Correspondingly, the inflicting of the death of God in the crucifixion of Jesus is not, in its deepest and controlling sense, to be seen in the plotting of the priests and in all the other machinations of petty power which bring Jesus to his cross. The causal connection of sin with the death of God is sin's requirement of the death of God for its absolving, such is sin's depth. This is seen not in the powers that be, but in the disciples. All the powers that be are needed for in this drama is to come on and be themselves. A walking-on part, requiring no rehearsal and drawing small pay. All they have to do is to eliminate Jesus in the way they eliminate any creative disturber of their anxious peace. The powers that be know nothing of the death of God. They merely keep it going. On the other hand, if we make the mistake of regarding fear and not guilt as the bottom line, the powers that be come nearer to the centre, for rulers are characteristically people easily afraid. I remember a powerful moment in a British television play when Jesus suddenly goes across to Pilate and whispers urgently in his ear: 'Don't be frightened! It's all right! Just stop being frightened!' Pilate pauses thoughtfully, then slaps Jesus hard across the face.[5]

Finally, the desertion of the disciples, Peter's betrayal and Judas' suicide have an important role in the larger context of their unique existential bewilderment. The situation spins them around like a top, and fear, which a scholastic would call the proximate cause of their behaviour, is a runner-up to guilt, which is the root of their condition. But fear is secondary. Just as it must not be allowed to promote the importance of Pilate, so it must not be allowed to confuse the importance of the disciples. Fear is not the ultimate human evil, ultimately because there is a God. So fear is not the bottom line of the great story, because this is the story of God.

Does this mean in the end that we are not all responsible for Jesus' death? Is this age-old belief, to say nothing of my last book, wrong? We are indeed responsible, but in a less dramatic and more real way than I there implied. As people involved in the primal guilt, we call, in a way we hardly understand, for the death of God.

[5] Dennis Potter, *The Son of Man* (London: Deutsch).

Perhaps the people most actively involved in any death significant of the death of God act more as functionaries of the deeper evil in all of us. The more apparently active, the more passive. The more apparently passive, the more active. In Eliot's *Murder in the Cathedral* it is the Women of Canterbury who elicit the deepest and subtlest awareness of complicity and guilt. The knights who *do* the murder are ham.

Epilogue

I said in the introduction: if I am intrigued and excited by my being to such an extent that I recognize in this passion something which is in all people everywhere and in every time, what must my real feeling be towards one who knows and wills what I can only be intrigued and excited by? For such a feeling 'dependence' is an inadequate and colourless name.

Of this feeling we can get only the faintest hints. Yet it is more worth the labour to name than any other. Wittgenstein said: 'Not how the world is, but that the world is, is the mystical.' There is however a step beyond this contemplative posture. Within the rapt unknowing that this posture maintains, there is sensed the one who knows. Within the ecstasy, there is sensed the one who wills. It is not a knowing that would collapse our unknowing. It is not a willing that would collapse joy into purpose. For it is not our knowing, it is not our willing, but of the one who is. That it is not our knowing or willing, that it is of another, is realized by this: the nearest we come to it is to be able to name the feeling with which our whole being yearns towards it.

What if that feeling were to be drawn out into a full conscious actuality? And what would draw it? What unimaginable condition of the universe would have it glow with its normally quite hidden fire and would have us aglow in its contemplation which would be more than contemplation, rather total assent? The unimaginable condition is Jesus risen from the grave of us who look and do not see. And we who saw him would be aglow with Holy Spirit.

Far more, and far more simple than the transfigured world of the poet and the visionary: far more, and far more simple than the angels Blake could see in an apple tree, this would be he, the one, who hides in the world and holds the heart in near but not total ignorance of its real feeling to him.

In the meantime let us attend to that feeling and seek to know its

149

name. The crucial question, the final question the quester for the Grail had to ask, was: Whom does the Grail serve? Ours is the same question, only interiorized at this end time. The beloved is named by the love that the beloved alone elicits: and we who are in that love must in the end give absolutely everything for it.

Appendix: What Is a High Christology?

There is a confusion over the meaning of the term 'a high Christology'. As used by New Testament scholars it means a description of Jesus by means of images which affirm equality with God. An example of a fully-fledged high Christology would be: 'In the beginning, before time began, the eternal Word was with God and was God. Two thousand or so years ago, this Word took flesh, was born of Mary, suffered and died for us, rose from the dead, and then returned to God whence he came.' The description depends, at its crucial points, on images. We are asked to imagine a 'time' before time began and a mysterious entity, in the presence of God and somehow identical with God (here the imagery significantly breaks down). We are asked to imagine this being 'taking flesh', suffering, dying, rising and returning in the flesh whence he came into the flesh.

By contrast, a 'low Christology' means a description of Jesus by images which do not evoke equality with God, such as 'Messiah-King', Christ, Son of Man, Angel, Son of David, the prophet who was to come into the world.

The confusion consists in equating those who expressed their belief in the former (Johannine) terms with 'believers in the divinity of Jesus, as subsequently defined at Nicaea'; while those who used the latter images are seen as 'people who did not believe in the divinity of Jesus, as subsequently defined at Nicaea'. That something is awry in these equations is indicated by the fact that Peter's sermons in the early chapters of Acts are certainly examples of a low Christology: 'Jesus of Nazareth . . . a man whose divine mission . . . God raised him from the dead . . . he has been raised to the right side of God and received from him the Holy Spirit . . . it is this Jesus that God has made both Lord and Messiah.' Yet Peter also says: 'There is no one else in all the world, whose name God has given to men, by whom we are to be saved.'

Here Peter is associating Jesus with the saving power of God in a unique way. In other words, something more is being attributed to, and expected from, this man from Nazareth with a divine mission, from this Lord-Messiah, than is ordinarily or obviously conveyed by such descriptions and titles. This 'more' shows up once attention is shifted from the titles and images as such to the sphere of attribution. This sphere brings into consideration the honour being paid to Jesus, the limitless belief in his power ('name'), the striking religious emphasis being given to a *man* in the context of a strict Jewish monotheism, the impression that he is constituting in practice a second religious focus in that tradition. It then becomes clear that the contrast observable in the quotations from Acts, between limiting titles and virtually unlimited attribution and expectation, is all over the New Testament.

What is attributed to and expected from Jesus in the New Testament goes far beyond what is 'ordinarily and obviously' conveyed by the titles. Those two adverbs point to an epistemological fact at the root of the problem of high and low Christology. This multiple fact can be expressed in three statements: (1) We cannot understand anything without forming images, nor can we communicate without pointing to images. (2) Images, which are the necessary condition of understanding, are not the sufficient condition. Understanding, and successful communication, only happen when people, while continuing to use the appropriate images, have got hold of something beyond the image and for which there is no image: they've 'got the idea'. A whole panoply of images will be assembled by a good history teacher, of land neglected or frivolously used, of half-starved peasants, of aristocrats, of a top-heavy royal court, of an expert banker racking his brains and wringing his hands; but there is no image for 'the causes of the French Revolution'. (3) When people argue, they are on the whole arguing not about the images they are using but about what they're getting at via the images. 'On the whole', for people wobble in such a way that the clever rhetorician can sway a debate or a court from its painful wrestle with some complex issue by producing a powerful and moving image. 'That's what we're really talking about!' people wrongly say to themselves.

I referred to 'appropriate' images, for an image serves its purpose of promoting understanding and communication only when it 'looks like', suggests, the idea one is trying to convey. The image cannot take you all the way, but it can and should point you in the right direction and give a friendly push. Think of the crucial role of new and felicitous images in the fantastic breakthroughs of modern astrophysics.

There are times when some big new idea is trying to emerge, when some unprecedented spiritual experience is flailing around, trying to find words. When this is happening, there will be a notable gap between the available images and the new idea. The gap that is always present and without which there is no understanding or communication is in this special case enlarged. All that can then be done, until some intrepid spirit produces some startling new image, is for the people involved to use the language of the accepted images and symbols and stretch it, try to use it to point to more than it normally does.

If there ever was a moment in human history which qualifies as such a critical time, such a watershed in religious consciousness, that moment is the birth of the Christian Era. We should expect to discern, in the primary documentation of that moment, multiple and heavy traces of the old and the new in tension, of something unheard-of seeking to come out of something heard-of from time immemorial, of a received religious language put to startling new use. That is exactly what we find. Peter's sermons in Acts are an example. What Jew had not heard of 'a man from Anathoth, or even Nazareth, with a divine mission'? What Jew had ever heard of depending on such a man for our ultimate salvation? In this matter of naming and enjoining the New Man, a correct epistemology generates what Newman called an antecedent probability which is abundantly verified.

I said that this 'enlarged gap' state of affairs would continue until some intrepid spirit tried to close the gap. This antecedent probability also is verified. The intrepid spirits were the members of the Johannine community whence came the fourth Gospel and the Johannine Letters. They produced a high Christology. Not only did their attribution-to, expectation-from and commending-of Jesus indicate his divine status, but their imaginal description of him also did so. Imaginal description was brought up towards the level of practical religious attribution. The person whom the latter honours as divine may be imagined as being up there in and with (again that strange wobble) God from all eternity, taking flesh as Jesus of Nazareth.

It is common knowledge that this high Christology prevailed in the Church, but the capital question is: What was the meaning of this prevailing? Does it mean that the Johannine people prevailed over all the low Christology people who, on the supposition I am attacking, did not believe in the divinity of Jesus, because they didn't image it but used an older language? Or does it mean that the images afforded by the Johannine people gave to people who had been getting along with a Son-of-Man Christology what they saw they needed to give clearer expression to the faith they had always held? If you're in the habit of treating a man as though he were God himself, it helps to be able to call him God. Bearing in mind the facts of epistemology and the uniquely revolutionary nature of the period that was putting such a strain on epistemology, the second alternative seems preferable.

There is strong subsidiary evidence in the fact that John's Gospel, the classic of high Christology, also contains some of the most primitive and low Christology to be found in the New Testament. If the high Christology had been felt by the author to be 'the real thing', the only appropriate way to confess Jesus, he would surely have ironed out those 'inadequate and misleading' descriptions of Jesus. On the contrary, he seems quite comfortable with them. It is certainly my experience that, once I had come to terms with a high Christology, I was able newly to enjoy the more primitive and partial descriptions of Jesus. Robert Heiler points out that it is characteristic of the most spiritually mature religiousness to readopt the more primitive religious language, of bloody sacrifice for instance, totally transforming it in the process. In the power of the end, the groping beginnings become newly precious. It could be that once one has taken responsibility for closing somewhat the image gap, one can let it open again with a new serenity in place of the tension with which it was first experienced.

The high Christology is in danger of forgetting that the gap is always there, for Christology and for all human knowing. There is the very human temptation to lean too heavily on the felicitous image and to behave mentally as though the truth could be imaged. The point where this temptation begins to run the high Christology into trouble has already been touched on twice. It is where we try to deal imaginally with 'the Word' in its original condition in John's Prologue. 'With' (or better 'towards', 'pointing to') 'God' and yet identical with God. How can we talk about this fullest implication of a high Christology: a divine being who is 'to-wards' God (otherwise how could Jesus have prayed?) but, being divine, must be God? Imaginally, it can't be done.

It is well known that the *homoousion* was *the* word of the high Christology people during the Nicene controversy. They were say-ing, in the strongest way they could think of, that Jesus was God: if you think of God as a sort of 'divine stuff ', then Jesus was of that very stuff. They were trying to take further the Johannine narrow-ing of the image-gap in order to close it completely, so that the image, the description, would itself carry that divineness of Jesus on which the Christian faith was centred. They sought to avoid the last-ditch ambiguity, of being towards God and being God, to state unequivocally Jesus' identity with God in a way the imagination can handle. Of one 'substance'. Of course a highly mysterious, spir-itual and ineffable 'substance'; but under cover of this philosophic mysticism the imagination gets what it wants.

As long as we try to perform the above mental feat we run into difficulties. When we try to state how God and Jesus are 'of the same stuff ', we may find ourselves saying that they are both 'made of it', like two men are both made of man-stuff; in which case we have two Gods. The alternative is to say that they don't divide the stuff: each is it wholly, but each manifests it differently; in which case we have the heresy called Modalism, 'Father' and 'Son' being aspects of God. This makes no sense of the dynamic interaction of Father and Son which is the very life and meaning of the New Testament.

Athanasius, the real genius and architect of Nicaea, understood, however implicitly, that what was wrong about the *homoousion* was not the term itself but the thinking of the *ousion* as 'a sort of divine stuff '. He saw that the error was the use of this language to effect final closure of the image-gap. He consistently avoided the conse-quences of this 'divine stuff ' thinking. He resolutely stopped short of any attempt to say 'just how' Father and Son were one, 'what it was like'. He avoided the very thing that the high Christology peo-ple tended to revel in, the envisioning of the sublime unity. He simply said: Whatever the Father does, that the Son does, except generate the Son; whatever the Father is, that the Son is, except the Father.

This looks and feels like a cheat or a trick. 'The whole point', 'the whole problem', is being evaded. The mind is being starved.

What is being avoided is in fact the impossible, the operation of the pretentious mystagogic imagination. 'The whole point', 'the whole problem', is what the latter wants to satisfy. What is being deprived is the imagination, which, at first supplying traditional images and requiring the attribution of divine honours (low Christology), then shortening the gap and providing creative new images suggestive of divine status (high Christology), has at last overstepped itself. The imagination therefore required to be cut back, in what looks like the first act of epistemological appropriation ever performed by the Church. Lonergan aptly described Nicaea as 'the Church coming to intellectual conversion'. He is also quite clear that this conversion is not that 'coming into mastery of a critical realism' which von Hügel enjoined on a man I once knew who had asked for advice on the pursuit of comparative religion studies. ('It is the absence of this in almost all modernists everywhere that is the fatal flaw, etc.' I quote freely.) One learns to think correctly long before one is able to spell out what is involved in this awesomely selective process. Athanasius's knack of never putting a foot wrong in this matter Lonergan calls 'dogmatic realism'.

Athanasius places all the emphasis on attribution: the Son does what the Father does. He thus picks up the same thought-process whereby the low Christology, in spite of its inadequate image-base, asserted in practice the divinity of Jesus. To this Son of David, Man from Nazareth with a divine mission, Christ, is to be attributed what is attributed to God alone. Thus attribution emerges as the great constant in Christian affirmation of the divinity of Jesus. In the low, primitive Christology, it leaps beyond an inadequate imagery. For the high Christology it is the inbuilt critique of a more adequate imagery which behaves as though it were totally adequate.

Nothing is more misleading than to describe Athanasius's Nicaea as the final triumph of a high Christology without further explanation. This 'triumph' involved the critique and pruning of the high Christology so that the earliest voice of the Church could sound in it, the voice which transformed the language of primitive Christology without altering its terms.

The relationship between low and high Christology will be misconceived until it is reviewed in the light of the facts of mental life. Otherwise the partnership of these two conceptual witnesses to faith will be obscured, and the language of takeover will be preferred. Yet the partnership is evident. Just as the Johannine Christology accepts as partner the most primitive Christology, so Nicaea, which goes further than John in stating the equality of Jesus with the Father, restores more actively than John the original reasoning of the believing soul (Jesus does what only God does for us, therefore he is God).

Precisely because they have to deal so much in the images, the symbols, the terms used, scholars are especially prone to that excessive leaning on the image which is the cause of all the trouble, whether in Christology or in a family row. Yet what kind of a faith can it be that 'terminates' in images? *'Actus autem credentis non terminatur ad enuntiabile, sed ad rem'*, as Aquinas says (2a 2ae 1, 2 ad 2).

Note

It is commonly said that at Nicaea the Church defined the divinity of Christ. Yet the Council, and all the lucubrations preceding and following it, seems to be talking not about the divinity or non-divinity of a historical man, but about the divinity or non-divinity of something called 'the Word'. All agreed that 'the Word' was beyond the human, but only some appeared to want to name 'the Word' God. Jaroslav Pelikan says something like: The Council is not so much asking 'Is Jesus divine?' as 'Is what Jesus *is* divine?' What does this mean? How is it that a council which is trying to deal with the problem of Jesus and is always understood to have been doing so should be primarily involved not with Jesus, but with a quasi-divine entity called 'the Word' and asking whether this 'Word' is divine or quasi-divine?

The first rational problem created by believing that a man is God is not 'how can a man be God?' but 'how can we think of him as God without becoming incoherent? How can we explain what we believe?' This is the shape the problem takes only when it is a problem created by faith. Faith, that formless, unconditional Yes to Jesus and his whole world as our salvation, is already there, thrusting towards whatever coherence it can achieve. The problem 'how can a man be God?' is not a faith-created problem, but the inquiry of a non-believer. Here too I suspect there is much confusion, in contemporary christological debate, of *fides quaerens intellectum* with *intellectus quaerens fidem*. They can never be the same.

157

How can we resolve our faith-created problem? Let us take our pre-human being, up there with God, 'towards' God and yet somehow 'God'. In what way are we to think of how such a being can be thought about coherently with God? The answer is: very modestly. You have got to de-immerse yourself in the image, of for instance rays proceeding from the sun; you have got to de-Johannize a bit, clip the Eagle's wings and say what faith has been saying, in some form or other and in many different forms, from the beginning: Jesus, the Jesus you have tried to lift imaginatively into God, is God only, and truly, because he does for us what only God can do.

What Nicaea is dealing with is not 'the divinity of Christ' but 'the way people had been trying to deal with the divinity of Christ for the previous three centuries'. What Nicaea tackles is the critical epistemological problem created by the zealous attempts of imagination to serve faith. Those attempts had already brought theologians a long way from the man of Galilee into the abstruse tangle of the mind that believes in him and tries to think. That tangled thinking was already in the clouds. What Nicaea had to do was to take it where it was, and land it.